BASIC
ECONOM[...]

TEACH YOURSELF BOOKS

BASIC
ECONOMICS

Frank Livesey

TEACH YOURSELF BOOKS
Hodder and Stoughton

To all the members of my family

First published 1987

Copyright © 1987
Frank Livesey

No part of this publication may be reproduced
or transmitted in any form or by any means,
electronically or mechanically, including
photocopying, recording or any information
storage or retrieval system, without either
the prior permission in writing from the publisher
or a licence, permitting restricted copying,
issued by the Copyright Licensing Agency,
33–34 Alfred Place, London WC1E 7DP.

British Library Cataloguing in Publication Data

Livesey, Frank
Basic economics.—(Teach yourself books).
1. Economics
I. Title
330   HB171

ISBN 0 340 41782 X

Printed in Great Britain for
Hodder and Stoughton Educational,
a division of Hodder and Stoughton Ltd,
Mill Road, Dunton Green, Sevenoaks, Kent,
by Richard Clay Ltd, Bungay, Suffolk.
Photoset by Rowland Phototypesetting Ltd
Bury St Edmunds, Suffolk

Contents

Introduction   vii

1 Economic Decisions   1
Alternative uses of resources. Decisions taken by households.
Decisions by producers. Decisions by governments.

2 Economic Resources   12
Human resources. Non-human resources. Mobility of
resources. Specialisation.

3 Money   26
The functions of money. Characteristics of money.

4 Demand   31
Demand by households. Other influences on demand. Market
demand curves.

5 Supply   44
Choice of market. Market supply curves. Costs, profits and
the supply curve.

6 The Interaction of Demand and Supply   55
Equilibrium price and output. Reallocation of resources. Price
elasticity of demand. Price elasticity of supply. Factor markets.

7 Alternative Economic Systems   70
Classification of economic systems. Free market economy.
Command economy. Mixed economies.

8 Firms and Industries   76
Private and public sectors. Private sector business organisations.
Public sector business organisations. Scale of firms.
Chain of production and distribution. Location decisions.

9 Competition and Monopoly   91
Forms of competition. The effects of competition. External
costs and benefits.

10   Labour and Employment   108
Supply curve for labour. Economics of training. Employee and
employer organisations.

11   Finance   120
Sources of finance for households. Sources of finance for
producers. Financial intermediaries. Sources of government
finance. Banking systems.

12   Income and Wealth Creation   130
The distinction between income and wealth. A simple model of
an economy. National income.

13   Economic Growth and Development   139
Expansion of economic capacity. Forms of economic growth.
Economic growth and economic development.

14   The International Economy   148
Exchange. Determination of the exchange rate. Balance of
payments. Barriers to trade.

15   International Economic Institutions   164
The contribution of international economic institutions. World
liquidity. Regional trade groupings.

16   Economic Performance   174
National income. Nominal and real national income. Standard
of living. Employment and unemployment. Inflation. Balance
of payments. Economic capacity. Equality. Overall performance.

17   Management of the Economy   191
Fiscal policy. Taxation. Government spending, taxation and
aggregate expenditure. Monetary policy. Prices and incomes
policies. Supply-side economics.

Further Questions   209

Index   211

Introduction

As the title *Basic Economics* indicates, this book is written for people with little or no formal education in economics. You may either be studying for an examination, such as GCSE, or you may simply be interested in increasing your understanding of economic events and affairs. But even if you have no formal education in economics, you no doubt have some economic awareness and understanding, since economics is concerned with people's behaviour in everyday life: earning a living, spending their income, etc. This book shows how an economist views these everyday activities.

In Chapter 1 we discuss the decisions taken by individuals and households, by producers and by governments. You may well have faced the first set of decisions that we discuss. These relate to the choice of job or occupation, to the division of an individual or household's income between spending and saving, and to the selection of goods and services to be bought.

At the heart of all economic decisions is a choice among alternative ways of allocating resources. So in Chapter 2 we examine the factors that determine the stock of a country's resources, and the utilisation of those resources. We show how the use of resources can be improved by specialisation. For specialisation to occur there must be a mechanism for exchanging the goods and services in whose production people specialise. Most exchange involves the use of money. Consequently in Chapter 3 we discuss the nature and functions of money.

The process of exchange involves millions of transactions between suppliers and purchasers, and we next explain how these transactions fit together. We examine the situation from the purchaser's viewpoint in Chapter 4, and from the supplier's viewpoint in Chapter 5. In Chapter 6 we discuss the interaction of the decisions and actions of purchasers and suppliers. This discussion will help you to understand the factors that influence the prices of products: why, for instance, diamonds are more expensive than water.

Up to this point in the book we have been mainly concerned with the situations which would apply in free market economies. But in Chapter 7 we widen our horizons by considering alternative economic systems. In some economies resources are allocated mainly via the price mechanism, whereas in other economies planning plays a much more important role.

Today most economies are mixed, resources being allocated partly via the price mechanism and partly by planning. These economies are also mixed in the sense that goods and services are supplied partly by private sector and partly by public sector producers. The activities of both sets of producers are considered in Chapter 8. The various methods by which these producers compete against each other, and the consequences of competition, are set out in Chapter 9.

Having discussed the provision of goods and services we consider in Chapter 10 another important aspect of producers' activities, the provision of employment. We examine the benefits and costs of employment, and show how workers respond to various types of reward.

In Chapter 11 we consider the sources of finance that are available to producers, to households and to government. We also examine the forms of saving undertaken by each group, and show how decisions taken by the three groups interact.

Having discussed the market for goods, labour and finance, we take the analysis a stage further by showing in Chapter 12 how the activities of households, producers and the government interact to create income and wealth. We introduce the idea of the national income, an indicator of economic welfare, and show why national income may change.

One measure of a country's income is the output of goods and services. The higher the output, the higher the national income. Output can be increased up to the limit set by the nation's economic capacity. Thereafter output can increase only if economic capacity expands. In Chapter 13 we show how this expansion might come about, and we explore the meaning of economic growth and development.

In Chapter 14 we widen our horizons even further as we examine various aspects of the international economy: exports, imports, the determination of exchange rates, the balance of payments, and barriers to trade; and in Chapter 15 we discuss the role of the major international economic institutions.

In Chapter 16 we explore a question that is frequently debated in the press and on television: Is the economy performing satisfactorily? In answering this question we must, of course, have in mind a list of performance indicators, and examples of these are set out in Chapter 16.

An important influence – for good or ill – on economic performance is government policy, and in Chapter 17 we explain how governments attempt to manage the domestic economy.

By the time you have completed this book you will understand how economic forces operate at various levels, and how these forces affect you: as a consumer, as a worker or as a student. (In order to test your understanding, each chapter contains a number of questions.) Understanding economics will help you to make more informed judgements about the policies adopted by firms and governments, and will equip you to make better decisions in important areas of your own life.

The first draft of the manuscript was read, as usual, by my wife Grace. The final draft was typed efficiently and cheerfully by Liz Campbell. I am very grateful to both.

1

Economic Decisions

Economics is concerned with human behaviour, with the factors that influence decisions, and with the consequences of these decisions. In this first chapter we examine the decisions taken by individuals and by groups of individuals.

We show that in virtually every economic decision, five elements can be found: choice, scarcity, opportunity cost, uncertainty and planning. You might not be aware that your own decisions can be described in these terms, but you will recognise that this is so as you read this chapter.

We discuss these elements as they apply to decisions taken by households, producers and governments. We are, of course, able to discuss only a few of the decisions taken by these three groups. But this discussion is sufficient to demonstrate the essential features of all economic decisions.

We first examine decisions taken by households relating to spending on housing and insurance, to the allocation of income between consumption and saving, and to the choice of job or occupation. We subsequently consider decisions by producers relating to the products to be supplied, and the resources to be used in supplying these products. Finally we discuss the factors that might influence government spending decisions, taking as an illustration the choice between spending money on building a stretch of motorway or on a hospital.

Alternative uses of resources

Economic decisions require a choice to be made between alternative uses of resources. Of the many decisions made by people each day, most relate to the use of resources and are therefore economic decisions.

A person reading the first page of this book while browsing in a booksellers has to decide whether to buy the book or whether to spend his or her money in some other way. A person who has already bought the book has to decide whether to use the next hour reading the book or watching the television or going for a walk. The decisions facing both these people are economic decisions, since they require the person to make a choice among alternative uses of resources: money in the first instance, time in the second.

In the above examples the decisions are taken by *individuals* acting as consumers. Individuals also make decisions as workers, as suppliers of finance, etc. Other decisions are made by *groups* of individuals. Families decide how to spend their time or money. The directors and senior managers of firms decide what products to supply. Governments decide what rates of tax to levy. These are all *economic* decisions.

The characteristics of economic decisions

In virtually every economic decision, five elements can be found:

1   *Choice*   The individual or group has to choose between alternative courses of action, between alternative ways of using resources.

2   *Scarcity*   The term 'scarcity' may conjure up visions of thirsty travellers searching for water in the desert, or commuters standing in a queue awaiting the arrival of a bus! But the term has a much wider application. Scarcity exists whenever resources are insufficient to meet all the possible uses to which they could be put.

3   *Opportunity cost*   When resources are used in one way, they cannot be used in any other way. Opportunity cost is the *maximum benefit* that could be obtained from another use of resources. The opportunity cost of buying this book might be the satisfaction you would have obtained from going to the cinema or having a meal in a café. The opportunity cost of spending an hour reading the book might be the feeling of well-being after an hour's exercise. It will be clear from this example that opportunity cost is a subjective matter: it varies from one person to another.

4   *Uncertainty*   In most instances we cannot be absolutely sure what the outcome of a decision will be. You hope that by reading this book you will improve your understanding of economics. I share your hope, but I cannot guarantee that outcome. Nor can you guarantee that you will enjoy a visit to the cinema or physically benefit from an hour's exercise (you might sprain your ankle).

5   *Planning*   Despite the existence of uncertainty, individuals and

groups try to plan their future activities, and most decisions are taken within the framework of a plan. As we shall see, in some instances planning can be a very complex process. In other instances the process is so simple that people do not realise that they are engaged in planning.

Having discussed the characteristics of economic decisions, we now examine some of the types of decisions taken by households, and consider how the decisions may be taken. We shall later examine decisions taken by producers and governments.

Decisions taken by households

Planning by households

Whether they realise it or not, all households make plans which guide their decisions. Some households make detailed plans. They write down the proportion of income allocated to expenditure on food, clothes, entertainment, etc., and record the amounts actually spent on each item. Other households have less detailed plans. They have more vague ideas about how much to spend on various products, and may never write these ideas down.

In planning their expenditure, households take into account their expected income. This means that they also have a plan relating to work and other ways of obtaining income.

Benefits and costs

In drawing up their plans, households take into account two sets of expected benefits and costs:

1 *Benefits and costs within the household* Some very important questions arise here:
(a) How much of the household's income should be spent on the husband, how much on the wife and how much on the children? (Parents are aware that it is possible to spend too much as well as too little on children.)
(b) How much time should the father and/or the mother spend earning money and how much time should they spend with their family, meeting their non-material needs?

2 *Benefits and costs to the community* In making decisions many households take into account the interests of other members of the community. An obvious example is charitable giving. Some households, following the biblical principle of tithing, give away a minimum of a tenth of their income. Other households do not have a

definite figure in mind, but expect to give some of their income in response to different appeals that are made.

Decisions on the use of time also affect other members of the community. There is a wide range of activities and institutions whose primary purpose is to benefit others: the 'meals on wheels' service for the elderly and disabled, the Samaritans who help people in distress, the volunteers who pick up the litter that can disfigure the countryside.

Planning and decisions

Plans therefore guide the decisions. Households try to ensure that their decisions are in line with their plans. But plans may be modified over time, for three reasons.

1   Additional information becomes available, from two sources:
(*a*)   Households learn from the decisions that they take. The benefits (or costs) of a decision may be as expected or they may be different from what was expected, as noted above. If a household obtains more pleasure than expected from spending money on a certain product, it may plan to spend more money on that product, and less on another product, in the future.
(*b*)   Households become aware of additional ways of using resources. They are introduced – perhaps by friends or through advertising – to other products which they can buy. They learn of new ways of spending their leisure time.

2   A change occurs not simply in households' awareness, but also in the actual range of uses to which resources might be devoted. Every week sees a change in the range of products offered by manufacturers, as new products are introduced and some existing products are withdrawn. A major disaster provides a new opportunity for charitable giving.

3   Households' objectives may change, quite independently of any of the factors considered above. Returning to the earlier example, a person who becomes a Christian and adopts the principle of tithing may revise his or her expenditure plans. (This may also occur if he adopts the biblical principle of fasting!)

Let us now examine the factors involved in household decisions concerning expenditure on two items: housing and insurance.

Expenditure on housing

Expenditure on housing is influenced by decisions relating to:

1   *Location*   The ideal location might be one near to work, school

and shops, well served by public transport and surrounded by green fields. In practice most locations are not ideal; a choice has to be made among locations which meet some of these needs but not others. (The opportunity cost of a location near to work and shops may be an absence of green fields.)

2 *Size and style of house* In deciding what size of house or flat to buy, account is taken of the current size of the household and of any likely future changes. If an increase in the size of household is anticipated, should a bigger house be bought now, at a higher price, or should the family wait until the extra room is needed and then move?

The style of house may depend partly upon the size, but a choice can sometimes be made among alternative styles: detached, semi-detached, terraced, bungalow, flat, etc. Moreover, some people may think it worth while paying for an individual style, while others may prefer a house that is part of a uniform estate.

3 *Buy or rent?* Some people might prefer to buy a house and others to rent. But the final decision will be heavily influenced by the relative costs of the two alternatives. Weighing up relative costs may not be as easy as it seems at first. The purchase price, the current rate of interest payable on a mortgage and the current rent will be known. But changes in mortgage rates and rents cannot be predicted precisely.

Uncertainty also surrounds the price at which the house can be sold in the future. In some years rapidly rising house prices have added more to house-owners' wealth than income from employment. In other years the price of houses has fallen.

4 *Size and type of mortgage* If it has been decided to buy the house, a further decision has then to be made as to what size of mortgage to seek. The higher the proportion of the total cost which can be borrowed via the mortgage, the more money the household has left to spend on other things. On the other hand, interest payments will be greater in future years. In making this decision, a view has to be taken about the household's pattern of income over time. If income is likely to increase, it may be best to take out a high mortgage. If income may decline (e.g. because of unemployment), a lower mortgage may be better.

There are different types of mortgage and these also have different patterns of interest payments.

> **Qu. 1.1** Imagine that you have just started work and have moved to a new town. What do you think would be your expenditure on housing in (*a*) your first, (*b*) your second year of employment?

It can be seen that a very large number of factors can influence expenditure on housing. Different decisions give rise to different 'bundles' of benefits and costs to the household, and also to the various members within the households.

Expenditure on insurance

When people take out insurance policies they are protecting themselves against the undesirable consequences of future events which may or may not happen. The firms offering insurance cover know from past experience the probability of such events occurring and therefore the amount that they are likely to have to pay out to meet claims. They charge premiums intended to cover these payments and yield a profit.

The majority of people pay out more in premiums than they receive in direct benefits. For a minority the reverse is the case. Insurance is a pooling of risks.

Risks for which insurance is available include:

(a) Damage to property and contents by fire.
(b) Theft.
(c) Personal accident.

In deciding whether to buy insurance cover, account should be taken both of the money that will be received in the event of a successful claim, and the consequences of not having cover. A person whose car is essential for getting to and from work would be more likely to insure his car against all risks than someone whose car is used only occasionally for leisure. (In most countries car owners are obliged by law to take out 'third party' insurance to meet the costs of damage caused to other vehicles.)

Similar principles apply to life *assurance*, but there is an important difference. The holder of a life assurance policy has the right to draw agreed benefits as they become due.

A choice is available between:

(a) With-profits and non-profits policies. The costs and benefits are higher for the former.
(b) Pure (or whole) life and endowment policies. With the former, payment is made at death; with the latter, payment is made after a specified number of years or at death if earlier.

Consumption versus saving

Household income is allocated between consumption and saving. The pattern of income, consumption and saving of every household varies over time. A fairly typical series of stages would be as follows:

1   Both husband and wife work; they borrow a large amount (via a mortgage) to buy a house; a high proportion of spending is on consumer durables (e.g. furniture) and on leisure activities.
2   Children are born, leading to additional needs for consumption and to a reduction in household income as the wife gives up work. Saving is very low, perhaps negative (i.e. the household finances expenditure by borrowing).
3   As the children grow up, further needs for expenditure arise (perhaps including a move to a larger house). But this may be balanced by additional income arising from:
    (*a*)   promotion obtained by the husband,
    (*b*)   the wife's return to work,
    (*c*)   the entry of older children into paid employment.
4   Children leave home, expenditure needs decline, while income remains stable or increases. Saving is at a maximum.
5   At retirement, income drops substantially and is supplemented by drawing on past savings.

In allocating its income between consumption and saving, each household should take account of the way in which its circumstances are likely to change over time. Some households may expect to follow the stages outlined above. Others may have different expectations: a wife may wish to return to work immediately after the birth of her children, for example.

The allocation decision will also be affected by the yield on saving and the cost of borrowing. (Various forms of saving and borrowing are outlined in Chapter 11.)

> **Qu. 1.2** How would you expect the pattern of expenditure of a household with several young children to differ from that of a retired couple?

Decisions relating to work and leisure

These decisions include:

1   *Choice of job or occupation*   The choice of job or occupation is strongly influenced by:
(*a*)   A person's natural abilities.
(*b*)   The cost and duration of training required.
(*c*)   Financial and non-financial rewards.
(*d*)   Working conditions.
Let us consider these factors with respect to two occupations: a doctor and a farm labourer.

The rewards enjoyed by a doctor are high. But to become a doctor one has to be strong academically. The number of places in medical colleges is much less than the number of people seeking admission, and successful applicants must have good school examination grades. The training period is long, and medical students, and indeed many doctors, have to work long hours, mostly indoors.

A person who is not academically inclined, who is unwilling to undertake extensive training, whose expenditure needs are modest and who likes to work in the open air, may choose to work as a farm labourer.

2   *Promotion*   In deciding whether to aim for promotion, both the benefits and costs should be considered. The benefits are a higher income and, usually, a more interesting job. The costs may include working longer hours, and moving home.

3   *Place of work*   Where a person works sometimes follows from the decisions discussed above. But even with a given occupation and promotion plan, a choice of working locations is often possible. The importance attached to this choice is illustrated by the fact that there are often job vacancies in some parts of the country, but unemployed workers who could fill those vacancies may prefer to remain in other parts of the country, for a variety of reasons.

4   *Hours of work*   How long a person works depends to some extent on legislation and social conventions relating, for example, to the minimum school-leaving age and the age at which state retirement pensions are payable. But individuals do make choices: whether or not to work overtime, whether to take early retirement, and so on. In making these decisions individuals take account of their expenditure plans. This again illustrates the interrelationships among the various decisions examined in this chapter.

> **Qu. 1.3**   What factors have influenced your choice of job or occupation?

Decisions by producers

Decisions by producers involve the five factors identified above: choice, scarcity, opportunity cost, uncertainty and planning. To avoid repetition we shall not discuss each factor separately. However, we do begin with a brief discussion of planning.

Planning by producers

In the one-man business, the plan may be in the head of the owner. In the large company or corporation, plans are thoroughly documented so that the activities of all sections of the company may be as well coordinated as possible. Firms monitor the outcome of their activities and compare this with the planned outcome. As examples of these activities we examine decisions relating to two areas: products supplied and resources used.

Products supplied
Producers are often motivated by a desire for:

(*a*)   security,
(*b*)   profitability,
(*c*)   growth.

In some instances all these objectives can be met by one plan, one set of decisions. If a producer can supply a product that meets a need not met by other producers, it may achieve higher sales, greater profits and hence increased security.

But in other instances there may be a trade-off among these objectives. Many new products fail. Producers often have to decide whether to introduce a new product, knowing that sales and profits could either rise or fall substantially, or to follow a safer path by continuing to produce existing products.

A number of factors may influence this decision:

1   *Size of firm*   Large firms often have an advantage over smaller firms in that they produce a wide range of products which provide a more secure base, enabling them to accept the risks involved in the introduction of new products.

2   *Profitability of existing products*   If the profitability of existing products is rising, there is less incentive to introduce new products. On the other hand if the profitability of existing products declines, the introduction of successful new products may be essential to the producer's survival.

3   *Legal status of producer*   Companies whose shares are freely traded and widely held may avoid risky decisions which could lead to a fall in profits. They might fear that lower profits would lead in turn to a fall in their share price, making the company vulnerable to a takeover bid. A producer whose shares are less widely held and whose activities are less widely publicised (e.g. a private company in the UK) may feel able to follow a more risky, but *potentially* more profitable, course.

State owned or controlled producers are usually more limited than other producers in the type of products they are allowed to supply.

4   *Type of product*   When a firm is considering adding a product to its existing range it often thinks first of a product which is related to its existing products because:

(*a*)   it uses similar resources or inputs (e.g. raw materials); and/or

(b)   it is sold into the same markets. Producers who manufacture machines for sale to other producers usually think first of adding new machines to their range. Producers who manufacture snack products for sale to consumers usually think first of new snack products.

However, when profits from existing products and markets are declining, producers may adopt an alternative strategy. They attempt to *diversify*, i.e. to produce different types of product and/or supply different markets.

Resources used

A second major set of decisions made by producers concerns the *resources* used. The most important general influence on the resources used by a producer is the range of products made. However, a given range of products can usually be made by alternative combinations of resources or *inputs*. The producer has to choose (a) the mix of resources (i.e. the relative quantities of labour, capital and land – see Chapter 3), and (b) the type of labour, capital and land.

For instance, the choice may be between on the one hand a large amount of labour, grouped in small units, using small tools, and on the other hand an assembly line, using automatic machinery, more land, less skilled and fewer workers. The choice will be influenced by:

(a)   The cost of the various inputs. As relative costs change, so do the preferred mix and type of input. For example, if wage-rates rise, capital is likely to be substituted for labour.
(b)   The productivity of the inputs.
(c)   The volume of output: in general, the higher the output, the more capital is employed per unit of labour.

> **Qu. 1.4**   Why might the actual outcome of a producer's activities differ from the expected outcome?

Decisions by governments

Yet again we find that decisions involve choice, scarcity, opportunity cost, uncertainty and planning.

Planning by governments

Planning by governments requires decisions to be made concerning total government expenditure, the pattern of that expenditure, and revenue from taxation and other sources. (These factors are discussed in detail in later chapters.)

The government or state is the single largest spender in many countries, and governments undertake a very elaborate planning process, as they try to reconcile the expenditure bids of different government departments or state agencies.

The planning process is complicated by the wide range of potential beneficiaries of government spending and the absence of a common measuring rod that can be applied to all forms of spending. This is in contrast to households, who might use personal satisfaction as the measuring rod, or producers who might use profitability.

To illustrate these characteristics of government planning, let us consider the issues involved in the choice between spending a given amount of money on building a motorway and a hospital.

The motorway would be expected to yield the following benefits:

(*a*) less congestion on existing roads;
(*b*) less damage from lorries going through towns;
(*c*) shorter journey times;
(*d*) lower transport costs for producers, leading to lower prices of products and/or higher profits;
(*e*) fewer accidents.

The hospital would be expected to yield the following benefits:

(*a*) shorter hospital waiting-lists, leading to
(*b*) fewer deaths, and
(*c*) fewer working-days lost through injury or illness; this would benefit both workers and employers.

The above lists are not comprehensive; for example, the employment effects of the two projects would also differ. But it is clearly a very difficult task to arrive at a decision as to which project should be undertaken. The beneficiaries differ, as do the forms of benefit.

> **Qu. 1.5** Explain why governments may find it difficult to choose between alternative forms of expenditure.

> **Qu. 1.6** How does government spending and taxation affect you?

2

Economic Resources

In the previous chapter we showed that economic decisions involve making a choice between alternative uses of resources. We examined decisions relating to the use of resources by households, producers and governments.

In this chapter we take more of a 'bird's eye view', seeking to answer two questions:

1 What factors determine the stock of a country's economic resources?
2 What factors influence the utilisation of these resources?

In considering these two questions, it is very helpful to *classify* economic resources. The first, very broad, distinction to be made is between human and non-human resources.

Human resources

The stock of human (and non-human) resources has two aspects: the volume or quantity, and the quality.

Quantity of human resources

Changes in the quantity of human resources, i.e. in the size of a country's population, are of two types:

1 *Natural changes* Natural changes in population reflect the balance between birth and death rates. Figure 2.1 shows how population tends to change as an economy develops. Greater medical knowledge, better nutrition and improved sanitation and hygiene cause the birth rate to rise and the death rate to fall. Consequently the population increases. Gradually the birth rate begins to fall, for several reasons:

(*a*) Improved living standards mean that families rely less on children as an insurance in old age.

(*b*) Increased opportunities for work and leisure make women more reluctant to spend a substantial part of their lives on rearing children.

(*c*) More reliable methods of contraception are introduced.

The fall in the birth rate means that the population begins to rise less rapidly. Eventually the point may be reached where the birth rate falls below the death rate, causing the population to decline.

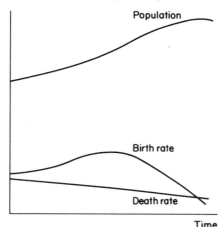

Fig. 2.1   Changing population

2   *Changes due to migration*   The population may change because of migration movements. Immigration causes the population to rise; emigration causes it to fall.

These movements occur because of perceived differences in the opportunities provided by different countries. The United States has received immigrants from many countries for various reasons: Jews have sought refuge from persecution, the Irish emigrated to escape from poverty and even death at the time of the potato famine, and people have left many other countries in the search for improved job prospects.

> **Qu. 2.1**   What changes would you expect to occur over the next fifty years in the population of any country with which you are familiar?
>
> **Qu. 2.2**   Explain why improvements in medical knowledge could cause a population to either increase or decrease.

Optimum population

Given the stock of other resources, the optimum population is the size of population at which the output of goods and services per head of the population would be maximised. Since the stock of other resources is constantly changing, the optimum population also constantly changes. As we shall see from our discussion of non-human resources, the stock of capital usually increases over time; consequently the optimum population tends to increase. On the other hand, if the stock of cultivated land does not change, an increase in population can lead to overcrowding and food shortages.

Quality of human resources

In economics the quality of resources is defined in terms of the contribution made by these resources to the output of goods and services. It should not be confused with other definitions of quality or worth.

Quality in the economic sense is determined by two factors:

1 *Inherent ability* Some people are born with abilities that fit them for particular tasks or occupations. Many labouring jobs require considerable strength; the assembly of electrical appliances often requires manual dexterity; a brain surgeon and a barman both require a steady hand.

2 *Acquired ability* People acquire the ability to perform certain jobs through education and training. The purpose of much education and training is to develop an inherent ability, and training would be useless in the absence of such an ability. For example, learning how to read music and spending hours a day in practice would not turn someone who is tone-deaf into a concert pianist. In fact it seems that few people have the natural ability required to become a concert pianist. Other jobs can be performed by more people of varying aptitudes, but who still require training. Drivers are a good example.

> **Qu. 2.3** What factors do you think might account for differences in the quality of the labour forces of Australia and Papua New Guinea?

Flow of labour inputs

This is the technical term used to describe the number of man (and woman) hours of work supplied in a given period. Several factors, other than the quality of labour, influence the flow of labour inputs derived from a given population.

Structure of population

The structure of population has two aspects:

1 *Age structure* People below a certain age are not usually capable of making a significant contribution to output, because of insufficient strength, lack of training, etc. Similarly the economic contribution of many people declines beyond a certain age as their physical or mental capacity deteriorates. Consequently the flow of labour inputs is likely to be greater, the greater the proportion of the population between the ages of, say, sixteen to sixty.

2 *Sex structure* Since women's employment is interrupted, however briefly, by the process of childbirth, the flow of labour inputs will tend to be lower, the higher the proportion of females in the population.

Legislation

Legislation can have a direct influence on the flow of labour inputs, as when the government imposes a minimum school-leaving age, or restricts the hours during which young people and women may work. Legislation can also have indirect effects. The provision of financial assistance to those not working may discourage people from seeking or remaining in employment. In many countries assistance is given to people not in employment because they are beyond a certain age, to those in full-time education, and to women who are about to have or have had babies.

Custom and tradition

Custom and tradition can have an enormous impact on the flow of labour inputs. We have noted that fewer inputs may be derived from women than from men because of biological factors and legislation. But probably an even more important factor is the custom in the country concerned. In many western and Asian countries married women have not been expected to work outside the home at least until their children grow up (although in the twentieth century attitudes have changed appreciably). On the other hand, in some African rural economies the women have traditionally done most of the manual work.

The number of hours worked during a person's lifetime is also influenced by custom and tradition. (Custom is often formalised by means of agreements between employers and workers.) In recent years many countries have experienced a reduction in the length of the standard working week, an increase in the number of holidays, and a reduction in the retirement age.

But vast differences remain between countries. Senior executives often retire at a later age in Japan than in the UK. In Europe one would not commonly see young children selling post cards to tourists as one does in Middle Eastern countries.

> **Qu. 2.4** If the size of the population of the UK remained roughly constant over the next twenty years how might the flow of labour inputs change?

Non-human resources

Two types of non-human resources can be distinguished: land and capital.

Land

As with other resources, land can be considered in terms of quantity and quality.

Quantity of land

In order to assess the quantity or volume of land possessed by a country, it is necessary to define 'land'. This may seem obvious, but in fact there are several definitions of land:

(a)   The total surface area of the earth, excluding that covered by water (oceans, lakes, rivers, etc.). By this definition very slight changes in the quantity of land may occur, such as by river erosion or by reclaiming land from the sea.

(b)   The total surface area of the earth, including dry land and water. By this definition the volume or quantity of land is fixed.

(c)   As (b), but including parts of the earth below the surface. Many extremely valuable resources (e.g. oil, coal, diamonds) are, or course, found below the surface. The quantity of those resources is constantly changing.

Flow of inputs

Land yields many different types of services or inputs. The wider the definition of land adopted, the greater the range of inputs. Taking the first definition of land given above, land is used by industry for building factories, by households for building houses and for recreation, and so forth. Moving on to the second definition, the sea is used for fishing, recreation and transport. Finally, moving to the third definition, land yields minerals, metals, and so on.

Quality of land

Different qualities or characteristics are required for different uses: fertility is obviously important for agricultural land, whereas flatness and the ability to take foundations are more important for land on which factories are built. Location is invariably important; for many purposes land in city centres is especially valuable. Many manufacturing industries are located near to water, which is used for cooling, for the discharge of effluent, etc.

In many instances the quality of land is *inherent*. This is obviously true of location, of deposits of minerals and metals and of topography (e.g. flatness). But in order to release the potential of these inherent qualities it is often necessary to apply a third type of resource, a third factor of production: capital. We discuss capital in detail below, but it is useful to give here a few examples of its application to land.

Land and capital

In order to bring oil to the surface, massive drilling rigs are often required. In order to mine coal, shafts have to be sunk and underground railways constructed. Land often has to be cleared and levelled before it can be used for building. Even the fertility of land is often improved by the application of capital in the form of fertilisers. Although we can make a distinction between land and capital, it is often difficult in practice to identify land as a separate factor or resource.

Capital

Capital is any resource or factor of production other than labour and land, that contributes to the production of goods and services. Note that this definition does not include money as such, even though individuals and firms may regard money as part of their capital assets.

This is an extremely wide definition, and various categories of capital can be distinguished.

Fixed and circulating capital

Fixed capital includes factory buildings, offices and machinery. Fixed capital remains distinct throughout its life (although it may be modified). It yields a flow of inputs or services over its life, and it gradually wears out through use or the passage of time. A turbine generates a given amount of electricity for a certain number of years (the amount declining as the turbine begins to wear out). A road is able to support a given number of vehicle-miles (the number depending on the weight of the vehicle) and then begins to crumble.

On the other hand *circulating* or *working capital* is incorporated into the product for which it is required. Textiles, wood and plastic are incorporated into furniture; diamonds and gold into jewellery; steel, plastic and rubber into cars.

Social capital

This refers to capital, often owned by the state, that makes an indirect contribution to the production of goods and services, or to economic welfare more broadly defined. Hospitals, schools, roads and prisons are examples of social capital. Thus, for example, hospitals (and medical facilities generally) aid the health and fitness of the working population; schools and other educational institutions impart skills which improve workers' productivity; roads are used in transporting goods between producers, and from producers to consumers; prisons increase the security of life and property.

Changes in the quantity of capital

We have shown that fixed capital assets gradually wear out and lose their value. Different assets have different life-spans. A machine may cease functioning after ten years whereas a factory may be occupied for a hundred years or even more.

This loss of value over time may be reversed if the demand for the services yielded by that asset increases. For example, an old run-down shop may become more valuable if the land on which it stands is required to build a modern shopping complex. Oil-bearing land shot up in value once a means was discovered of extracting the oil. A machine's value may increase if it can be used to manufacture a newly developed product.

But these are exceptions to the general tendency for the quantity of capital to wear out, to *depreciate* over time. To compensate for this depreciation new assets must be purchased (or existing assets repaired) if the quantity of capital is to be maintained.

Investment

Investment is expenditure on the purchase (or repair) of capital assets. In principle, total or gross investment can be divided into two parts, so that:

Total investment = replacement investment + net investment

If total investment exactly balances depreciation, i.e. if all investment is replacement investment, net investment is zero. In this situation the quantity of capital is unchanged. If total investment exceeds depreciation, net investment is positive and the quantity of capital increases. If total investment is less than depreciation, net investment is negative and the quantity of capital decreases.

In any given period of time the capital of some firms and households is likely to increase while that of other firms and households is likely to decrease. But for the economy as a whole, net investment is usually positive and the quantity of capital grows year by year.

> **Qu. 2.5** Explain the relationships between total investment, replacement investment, net investment and changes in the quantity of capital.

Quality of capital

We said in the previous section that when investment equals depreciation the quantity of capital is unchanged. Moreover, in some instances the quality of the capital stock is also unchanged (e.g. when raw materials are used and replaced by identical materials). Similarly, it is said that when the men painting the Forth railway bridge in Scotland reach one end of the bridge, they immediately begin painting at the other end; in this way the paintwork on the bridge is maintained at a constant quality.

But in many instances investment involves an increase or improvement in the quality of capital. This is because a later *vintage* of asset is installed. If a machine is replaced after ten years, the new machine is likely to have advantages over the previous one (e.g. it may run at a faster speed, incorporate more automatic devices and be easier to operate).

You sometimes hear people say that 'they don't make things like they used to do'. By this they usually mean that modern products are of a lower quality. While this may be so in some respects, the reverse is true in other respects. If you replace a ten-year-old car by a new one, you may expect the new one to be easier to drive, have better fuel economy and probably to be more comfortable.

As with other resources, the contribution of capital to output depends upon both quantity and quality.

Mobility of resources

We have shown that the output of goods and services is determined by both the quantity and the quality of economic resources. A third determinant is the *mobility* of resources.

Mobility can be viewed at various levels:

International mobility

Land
Land is completely immobile internationally (although commodities produced from the land are traded internationally). Differences in the quality of land in different countries help to explain the international pattern of production. Islands and other countries with long coastlines often have big fishing fleets, while South Africa, with its mineral resources, is the world's largest producer of diamonds.

Labour
As we saw earlier, labour is sometimes mobile internationally, although only a very small proportion of the labour force emigrates in any year.

Capital
The most mobile factor or resource is capital. Machines, vehicles and raw materials are produced in one country for use in another. A great deal of investment is undertaken by multinational companies whose activities are discussed in Chapter 8.

Mobility within an economy

There is greater *geographical mobility* within the national than the international economy. But geographical mobility is sometimes less important than *mobility between alternative uses*.

Mobility of labour
Two sources of labour mobility are shown in Figure 2.2.
1   *Entrants and exits*   The composition of the labour force constantly changes as some people leave and others enter. Examples of entrants and exits are given in Figure 2.2. Overall the skills and abilities of those who enter are likely to differ from the skills of those who exit. Thus the work force is adapted to a new mix of occupations. When countries develop rapidly, massive shifts in skills and abilities occur in a few generations. Skills that are needed for agricultural occupations decline and those required for manufacturing increase.
2   *Training and experience*   Individuals develop new skills by training and experience. The proverb says that to change one's horse in mid-stream is dangerous, but technological change is requiring more people to change their jobs or occupations. An unwillingness or inability to undertake re-training may be even more dangerous than attempting to change one's career.

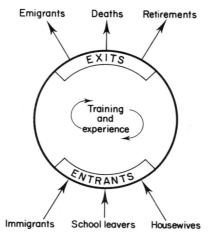

Fig. 2.2 Changes in the composition of the labour force

Mobility of land

In some instances the mobility of land *between uses* is high. Agricultural land may be used in the production of different crops, either as part of a regular policy of rotation or in response to changes in the profitability of these crops.

In other instances there may be barriers to the mobility of land. Once land is built on, it is costly to change its use. Considerable expense is involved when land that has been used for open-cast mining is returned to agricultural use, for example.

Mobility of capital

Capital is like labour in that mobility between uses of the total capital stock occurs (*a*) as some capital wears out and capital of a different type is installed, and (*b*) some capital assets are converted to a different use.

The opportunities for conversion differ from one type of capital to another. A building may begin life as an office block and subsequently be converted for use as an educational institution or a warehouse. On the other hand, a plastic extrusion machine is used for its original purpose throughout its life.

Qu. 2.6 'Land has no legs and therefore cannot be mobile.' Discuss.

Qu. 2.7 Is it sensible to talk about the mobility of fixed capital?

Specialisation

The term specialisation refers to the fact that resources are devoted to particular uses. For example, some people work on a vehicle assembly line, others drive the lorries and cars that are produced on that line, others treat the victims of accidents caused by those vehicles. Although, as noted above, mobility of factors is often desirable, specialisation leads to an increase in productivity, i.e. it enables a greater quantity of goods and services to be produced with a given quantity of resources. There are two sources of the increase in productivity: *comparative advantage* and *learning*.

Comparative advantage

If we take labour as an example, we can show that output is maximised when workers specialise in those occupations to which they are best suited. In primitive societies two common occupations are hunting and fishing. Let us suppose that if two men, John and Michael, spent half of their time hunting and the other half fishing, their weekly catches would be as follows:

	Animals	Fish
John	5	140
Michael	12	60
Total	17	200

If, on the other hand, they specialised in the activity to which they were best suited, the total output would be 24 animals (caught by Michael) and 280 fish (caught by John). Even if one person has an *absolute advantage* over the other in both activities, output will be increased if they specialise in accordance with the principle of comparative advantage.

	Animals	Fish
Fred	20	150
Bill	10	140
Total	30	290

The above table shows what the output would be if each person spent half his time in hunting and half in fishing. It can be seen that Fred is slightly better than Bill at fishing, but much better at hunting. Fred has a *comparative advantage* in hunting and Bill has a comparative advantage in fishing. If Fred spent four-fifths of his time in hunting and one-fifth in fishing, and Bill spent all his time fishing, the output would be:

	Animals	Fish
Fred	32 (= 4/5 of 40)	60 (= 1/5 of 300)
Bill	0	280
Total	32	340

If, to survive, Fred and Bill require both animals (for clothing) and fish (to eat), specialisation must be accompanied by exchange, a point discussed in detail below.

The principle of comparative advantage applies in modern as well as primitive societies. A successful businessman might be a very skilful driver, but it would pay him to hire a less skilful driver as a chauffeur, while the businessman spent the time thinking of ways of increasing the profitability of his business.

The principle also applies to other resources, such as the use of fertile land for agriculture, land in sunny seaside locations for tourism, and so forth.

Specialisation can apply at every level of the economy: within the household, within the firm, between firms, and between countries.

Learning

The second reason why specialisation increases productivity is that it enhances learning. The greater the degree of specialisation, the more quickly do workers learn to master their jobs.

This principle operates to the fullest extent when operations are broken down into very small units. For instance, on a vehicle assembly line the task performed by a worker may last for only a few seconds (e.g. tightening the bolts on a wheel using a power-tool). Consequently the task can be learned very quickly.

The disadvantage of a very high degree of specialisation is boredom and a loss of job satisfaction. This may be a cost to the workers only. But if it results in high absenteeism and labour turnover it counteracts the economic advantages of specialisation.

> **Qu. 2.8** How can the principle of comparative advantage help to explain (*a*) international specialisation, (*b*) specialisation within the household?

Exchange

As noted above, specialisation must be accompanied by exchange:

(*a*) Within the *household*, economic exchange involves the provision of services by the different members. For instance, mum might do most of the household chores while dad might be the main income-earner. But the family is more than an economic unit. Families are bound together by affection which does not depend on economic motives; they exchange more than economic services.

(b) Within the *firm*, exchange is primarily economic in nature. Shareholders buy shares in the hope of obtaining a satisfactory dividend; employees work for a wage or salary. But non-economic motives may also be important. Workers are influenced in their choice of jobs not only by the rate of pay but also by how they 'get on with' their colleagues.

(c) At the national level, exchange *between firms* is extremely important. The process of production and distribution has a number of stages, and different firms are often involved at each stage. Figure 2.3 shows one (highly simplified) possible pattern relating to washing machines.

There are several suppliers of raw materials (e.g. iron ore, oil, timber). These materials are supplied to firms which incorporate them into various components: steel doors, plastic mouldings, motors, dials, etc. These components are supplied to firms who assemble the washing machines. They are then transported to distributors who stock and display them. (Washing machines are usually transported direct from the assembler to retailers, but many products are handled by wholesalers who subsequently sell them to the retailers.)

(d) Finally, exchange takes place *between countries*. Countries that grow oranges or manufacture computers supply these products to countries that do not produce them.

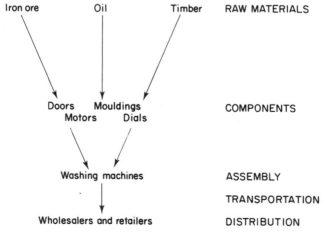

Fig. 2.3 Production and distribution of washing machines

Forms of exchange

There are two forms of exchange:

1 *Barter* Barter occurs when two products are exchanged directly for each other. If this was the only form of exchange, specialisation would be severely limited since exchange or trade would occur only when there was a *double coincidence of wants*. A person who spent all his time making clothes would be able to obtain food only when he found someone who wanted the particular jacket or shirt that he had made or could make. Under such circumstances very few people would take the risks involved in specialising as a tailor.

2 *Exchange using money* A *medium of exchange* is a commodity which is desired not for use but because it is generally accepted in payment for other commodities that are desired for use. The term 'money' is given to such a commodity. When commodities are supplied for money a double coincidence of wants is no longer necessary for exchange. A tailor can sell a jacket knowing that the money he receives will be accepted for payment for his needs: food, fuel, etc.

Countertrade

Given the advantages, it is not surprising that money is used for most exchanges or trade. But when money is scarce, barter may be used. In recent years international trade has been characterised by an increase in countertrade, one form of which is barter. For example, 100 000 tonnes of New Zealand lamb was exchanged for 6 million barrels of Iranian oil in a deal valued at $160 million. In other forms of countertrade, a purchase is conditional upon at least part of the cost being offset by purchases or other financial assistance by the seller country.

> **Qu. 2.9** Explain what is meant by: (*a*) investment, (*b*) depreciation, (*c*) social capital, (*d*) exchange.
>
> **Qu. 2.10** Discuss the proposition that all exchange is undertaken for economic motives.

3

Money

The functions of money

We saw in the previous chapter that money is the term given to any commodity that is generally acceptable in exchange for goods and services, i.e. it acts as a *medium of exchange.*

Money also acts as a *store of value.* Indeed, if it did not do so, its function as a medium of exchange would be seriously hindered. People would be reluctant to accept, in payment for goods supplied or services rendered, a commodity whose value might decline substantially.

Closely connected with this is money's function as a *unit of account*, a common measuring rod. If pineapples sell for £1 and peaches for 20 pence, we know that in the eyes of purchasers a pineapple is worth five peaches.

For many transactions payment is immediate, but for some it is deferred. Goods are bought on credit; a loan is made and interest payments are made subsequently. Consequently money acts as a *standard of deferred payment.*

Qu. 3.1 List the main functions of money.

Forms of money

In modern economies paper is the most important form of money, the paper being imprinted with the appropriate photographs, pictures, words or numbers. Metals are also a common form of money. Other commodities that have been used as money include seashells, beads and cigarettes. Cigarettes were used quite widely as money in Germany in the days immediately after the end of the Second World War, and today they are used – unofficially – as money in some prisons.

Characteristics of money

Any commodity that is used as money should ideally have the following characteristics:

1 *Stable stock* The stock of money should not vary markedly over time. One reason why precious metals have been used so frequently is that although the current output may change as fluctuations occur in mining activity, these changes in output lead to only small differences in the stock which has been built up over many years. Sometimes rapid changes in stocks have occurred, as in the sixteenth century when European countries obtained vast quantities of gold (sometimes illegally) from other continents. The result has been a fall in the value of money or, putting the matter another way, a rise in the price of goods, a process known as *inflation*.

In principle it would be easy to increase the stock of paper money, but governments attempt (not always successfully) to limit increases. The main purpose of government control is to prevent rapid inflation.

2 *Durability* Metals are more durable than many other commodities; coins last much longer than sea shells or cigarettes. It sometimes happens that low-denomination bank notes are replaced by coins because of the greater durability of the latter. (Many transactions involve the use of cheques. The fact that cheques are not durable does not matter, since each cheque is used for only one transaction.) The need for durability rules out a large number of commodities, including most foods, for use as money.

3 *Portability* Here the balance of advantage as between metals and paper changes. It is usually easier to carry a given amount of money in bank notes than in coins, although this obviously depends upon the respective denominations. Again, many products are ruled out by the need for portability. Bricks are very durable but would not be easy to carry around (nor would their stock be easy to control).

4 *Homogeneity* All items of money of a given denomination should be virtually identical. All pound coins are alike except, of course, that some are more worn than others. On the other hand there are considerable differences in diamonds of a given size. Consequently although diamonds may be valuable, they would not be very suitable as money.

Qu. 3.2 Explain why the following would not be very suitable as money: (*a*) coconuts, (*b*) bananas, (*c*) diamonds.

Qu. 3.3 Why do you think governments often have the ultimate responsibility for the control of the stock of money? Do you see any dangers in this?

Money and credit

In order to understand the difference between money and credit, consider a man who, on his way home from work at the end of the week, buys a toy for his young son. He might pay for the toy in one of several ways:

(a)   If he has received his wages in cash he might use bank notes or coins.

(b)   If his wages have been paid into his bank account he might write out a cheque.

(c)   He might write out a cheque, but this time using an overdraft granted by his bank.

(d)   If he knows the shopkeeper well he might be allowed to take the toy home on condition that he pays within a week.

In the first two instances the man uses money to purchase the toy. In the last two instances he uses credit, because in effect he has borrowed money which he will subsequently have to repay (to the bank or to the shopkeeper). Another way of putting this is that money and credit are both assets, but credit as an asset is matched by a liability.

Qu. 3.4 Distinguish between money and credit.

Creation of credit

The primary functions of banks are to accept deposits and to make loans or investments of one kind or another. In this process of taking and investing deposits, banks increase the total amount of credit (and therefore total spending power). This is most easily understood by considering the activities of the earliest ('primitive') banks.

Primitive banks

It was essential that the early banks could offer security for cash or other valuables deposited with them. They required a vault or safe (together with a reputation for honesty). Consequently many early bankers were goldsmiths who had vaults in which to keep their own gold.

People deposited their cash for safekeeping on the understanding that they could withdraw the cash on demand. However, the bankers gradually learned that only a small proportion of their depositors wished to withdraw their cash on any one day. Most of the cash simply lay idle in the bank vaults.

The more enterprising bankers realised that they could put this idle cash to good use. They could lend it out at interest. For example, experience might reveal that the maximum proportion of deposits withdrawn on any day was 2 per cent. Allowing a margin for error, this might suggest that if the banks retained 10 per cent of the deposits in their vaults they would always be able to meet depositors' demands for repayment. They would be able to lend the remaining 90 per cent.

For example, money deposited by farmers might be loaned to manufacturers to purchase raw materials. This is the situation at stage 1 of the table below. £10 000 has been deposited, of which the banks have retained £1000 and loaned £9000.

As the manufacturers spend the £9000 that they have borrowed, the money finds its way back to the banks. For example, the manufacturers might pay farmers £9000 for wheat for making bread, leather for shoes, wool for clothing, and so forth. The farmers deposit this £9000 with the banks.

The new situation is as shown at stage 2 in the table. Total deposits are now £19 000, comprising the initial deposits of £10 000 and the *created deposits* of £9000. The banks' assets are also £19 000, comprising £10 000 cash and £9000 loans.

The creation of credit

	Bank liabilities (£000s)	Bank assets (£000s)	
Stage 1			
Initial deposits	10	Cash	1
		Loans	9
			10
Stage 2			
Initial deposits	10	Cash	10
Created deposits	9	Loans	9
	19		19
Stage 3			
Initial deposits	10	Cash	10
Created deposits	90	Loans	90
	100		100

Note that at stage 2 the banks' cash holdings are over 50 per cent of the deposits, well above the minimum ratio that the banks feel it is safe to maintain. Consequently, in order to increase their profits the banks will try to make further loans. Provided that the money loaned is always re-deposited, the final situation will be as shown at stage 3 in the table. Total deposits and assets are £100 000, and the £10 000 cash held by the banks is 10 per cent of total deposits.

Modern banking systems

There is one important difference between modern banking systems and the primitive system described in the previous section. Today banks usually create credit not by lending the actual cash that has been deposited with them, but by means of 'book entries'. For example, a bank might grant an overdraft facility to Autovehicles, a car manufacturer. When Autovehicles buys components from another manufacturer, Carparts, it pays by cheque. When the cheque is 'cleared' the amount will appear as a debit to Autovehicles's account and a credit (deposit) to Carparts's account. Bank deposits are now the major form of money.

However, although the mechanics of the two systems differ, the underlying principles are the same. Banks are able to create credit and deposits because only a small proportion of these deposits are converted to cash on any one day. Banks are, of course, capable of misjudging the situation, and there have been some spectacular bank failures. These failures have mainly occurred because the banks have maintained too large a proportion of their assets in illiquid forms (e.g. property), and consequently have been unable to meet depositors' demands.

Moreover, some banks are more successful than others in attracting deposits. The more deposits an individual bank attracts, the more loans that bank is able to make. In recent years there has been increasing competition, both in attracting deposits and in making loans, between banks and also between building societies and other financial institutions.

Qu. 3.5   Explain the banks' role in the creation of credit.

Near-money

There are various assets which can be converted very quickly into money and which are therefore classified as near- or quasi-money. They include building society deposits and shares, deposits with instalment credit finance companies, and securities held by institutions, such as bills of exchange.

It is becoming increasingly difficult to draw the line between money and near-money. For example, some building society accounts offer cheque books which can be used in the same way as the cheque books issued by banks.

Qu. 3.6   In what ways do banks and building societies seek to attract (a) lenders, (b) borrowers?

Qu. 3.7   What developments do you foresee in the supply of money and near-money over the next twenty years?

4

Demand

In previous chapters we have referred to the transactions that take place between suppliers and purchasers. In most countries literally millions of these transactions occur every day and we shall now see how these transactions fit together.

This explanation extends over several chapters. We examine the situation from the purchaser's viewpoint in this chapter and from the supplier's viewpoint in Chapter 5. In Chapter 6 we discuss the interaction of the decisions and actions of purchasers and suppliers.

Demand by households

We begin this examination of demand by discussing the factors which influence demand by households. For most of the section we look at the situation through the eyes of an individual consumer, but it should be remembered that a consumer is often making purchasing decisions on behalf of others in the household or family.

Planning by households

We showed in Chapter 1 that households plan their expenditure. Some plans are long term, others are much shorter term. Since there is not sufficient space to discuss all these plans in detail, let us concentrate on the planned weekly purchases of food by one housewife, Mrs Brown. We assume that Mrs Brown has already decided what her total spending on food will be, i.e. she operates within a *budget constraint.* This planned spending takes account of the household income and of the requirements of the various members of the household for both food and non-food items.

Alternative plans

In deciding how to spend the money that has been allocated to food,

Mrs Brown takes into account the need to provide both nutrition and enjoyment (sometimes there is a trade-off between the two, especially where children are concerned!).

There are usually alternative ways of meeting these needs, and when Mrs Brown sets out to do the shopping she will have in mind several alternative plans. She may, for example, have decided that the family will have *either* meat *or* fish on five days, *either* potatoes *or* rice on six days, fruit on three or four days, and so forth.

There would be no point in trying to formulate a single 'best' plan because she does not at this stage have the required information. She cannot be *certain* what products will be available, and what their quality and price may be. Her previous week's shopping will be a good but not a perfect guide, since changes may occur from one week to the next, and indeed from one day to the next. (Even if Mrs Brown goes to the shops with a clearly preferred pattern of expenditure in mind, she will be prepared to modify this pattern, i.e. to *revise her plan*, if the availability, quality and price of products are not as she expected.)

Price and quantity demanded

We can illustrate Mrs Brown's situation by reference to her demand for potatoes. Given the price that she last paid, and bearing in mind any information that she has subsequently received from friends, advertisements, etc., she might expect the price of potatoes to be 12 pence a pound. At this price she plans to buy 8 lbs. But she would also give some thought to what she might do if prices turn out to be different from this. At higher prices she would buy fewer potatoes (and more rice), at lower prices she would buy more potatoes (and less rice), i.e. *the quantity demanded varies inversely with the price.*

Demand schedule
Mrs Brown's intentions at this stage can be expressed formally as a demand schedule as shown in the table below.

A demand schedule for potatoes

Price (pence per lb)	Quantity demanded (lbs per week)
10	12
11	10
12	8
13	6
14	5

Demand curve

Mrs Brown's buying intentions can also be illustrated by means of a demand curve, as shown in Figure 4.1, which is based on the data in the table on page 32.

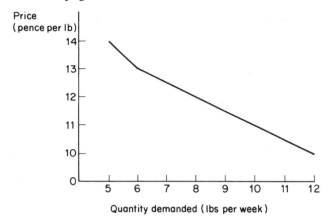

Fig. 4.1   Demand curve for potatoes

Other influences on demand

Figure 4.1 illustrates Mrs Brown's buying intentions given her perceptions, derived from past experience, of all the other factors that influence demand. If these perceptions do not change when she enters the shops, her initial expenditure plan will be implemented, i.e. she will buy 8 lbs of potatoes at a price of 12 pence.

However, if her perception of any of these other influences changes, she may modify her plan. The most important of these other influences are discussed below.

The price and availability of substitutes

To simplify the argument let us assume that for Mrs Brown rice is the only acceptable substitute for potatoes. The demand curve for potatoes, Figure 4.1, incorporates her expectation of the price of rice, say 40 pence a pound.

If, when she gets to the shops, she finds that rice has risen in price to 50 pence a pound, she may decide to buy less rice and more potatoes, i.e. to substitute potatoes for rice. If she finds that the local shops have run out of rice, she is likely to buy even more potatoes than she had planned.

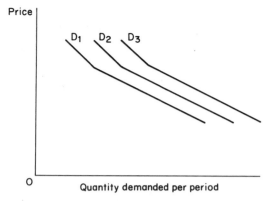

Fig. 4.2 Higher demand for potatoes

This change in intentions is illustrated in Figure 4.2. D_1 indicates the initial demand, at various prices, for potatoes, given the expectation that rice would be available at a price of 40 pence a pound. D_2 indicates the demand when she finds that the price is 50 pence, and D_3 the demand when no rice is available. Mrs Brown buys more potatoes, at any given price, than she initially intended.

Figure 4.3 illustrates the reverse situation, where rice is cheaper than expected. Mrs Brown substitutes rice for potatoes and buys less potatoes, at any given price, than she initially intended.

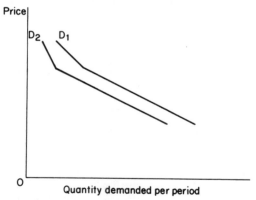

Fig. 4.3 Lower demand for potatoes

Qu. 4.1 Explain the meaning and significance of substitution.

Availability and price of complements

A favourite dish of the junior members of the Brown family is jacket potatoes with cheese, i.e. potatoes and cheese are complementary products. If Mrs Brown discovers that her local shops are offering cheese at a specially low price, she may decide to have jacket potatoes twice instead of once that week, i.e. her demand curve for potatoes shifts to the right. On the other hand, if she finds that cheese has shot up in price, she may decide that the children will have to go without their favourite dish this week, i.e. her demand curve for potatoes shifts to the left.

Quality

At certain times of the year the quality of potatoes may vary substantially from one week to another. If Mrs Brown finds that potatoes are of poorer quality than she expected, she may buy less than she intended. If their quality is higher than expected, she may buy more.

There may come a point where the quality is so different that we need to think in terms of different products, e.g. new as compared to old potatoes. We then have two different demand curves, rather than a shift of an existing curve.

So far we have been discussing factors which might cause expenditure plans to be revised in the short term. If we take a longer time perspective, two more influences on the demand curve for potatoes can be identified.

Income

We said above that Mrs Brown had already decided what her total spending on food would be, i.e. she is operating within a budget constraint. If income turns out to be different from what was expected, her budget constraint changes. In fact, when we are considering weekly purchases, it is unlikely that income will turn out to be different from what was anticipated when her provisional spending plans were formulated. This does sometimes happen, as when workers are suddenly made redundant or win the football pools. But generally, the main impact of unexpected changes in income – from whatever source – will be on longer-term plans, such as spending on the family's annual holiday or the purchase of consumer durables (e.g. washing machines or refrigerators).

Normal goods
If income is higher than expected, this will cause an increase in

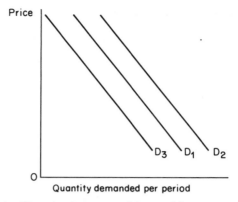

Fig. 4.4   Changing income and demand for a normal good

planned expenditure on most products, as shown by the shift of the demand curve from D_1 to D_2 in Figure 4.4. Conversely, if income is lower than expected, planned expenditure on most products will fall (D_3). When demand responds to a change in income in this way, the products concerned are termed *normal goods*.

Inferior goods

In some instances demand may not change in the way outlined above. When income turns out to be higher than expected, the planned expenditure on some products falls; this is shown by the downward shift of the demand curve from D_1 to D_2 in Figure 4.5.

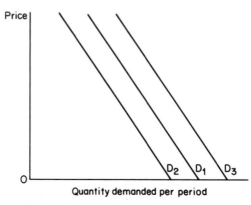

Fig. 4.5   Changing income and demand for an inferior good

Conversely, when income is less than expected, demand rises (D_3). When demand responds to changes in income in this way, the products concerned are known as *inferior goods*.

This may seem to be a strange outcome, and in order to help us to understand why this might happen, let us return to Mrs Brown's spending on potatoes. We consider first what might happen if, after Mrs Brown has made her spending plans, Mr Brown hears that he has won a prize on the pools.

Mr and Mrs Brown might decide to do what they had always wanted to do but could not previously afford, namely to eat more frequently at local restaurants. This would mean that Mrs Brown would buy less food to eat at home. Moreover, it is likely that her pattern of spending on food would change. She would probably spend more on ready-prepared 'convenience' meals and less on dishes that require more work, such as peeling potatoes. In other words the increase causes Mrs Brown to substitute other products for potatoes; her demand for potatoes falls.

Now let us consider what might happen if Mr Brown suddenly received notice of redundancy. Although he would hope to find another job, the first reaction of the family would be to try to cut down on their expenditure. One way of doing this would be to buy less meat and fish, and *more* potatoes. A jacket potato might become the main course four times rather than once a week.

If households reacted to changes in income in the way described above, the demand for potatoes would vary inversely with income and potatoes would be an inferior good.

> **Qu. 4.2** How might the demand for bread be affected by (*a*) a fall in the price of potatoes, (*b*) an increase in income, (*c*) the introduction of an improved 'bread-mix' for making bread in the home?
>
> **Qu. 4.3** How would you expect a sustained increase in income to affect the demand for
> (*a*) public transport,
> (*b*) holidays abroad,
> (*c*) housing?

Income elasticity of demand

The income elasticity of demand (IED) provides a more precise measure of the response of demand to a change in income. The table below shows how the demand for several products changes when income turns out to be £120 rather than £100 a week.

Quantity demanded

Income (£)	Product A	Product B	Product C	Product D	Product E
100	100	100	100	100	100
120	140	120	110	100	95
IED	2	1	0·5	0	−0·5

Income elasticity of demand is defined as the proportionate change in quantity demanded divided by the proportionate change in income:

$$\text{IED} = \frac{\Delta Q}{Q} \div \frac{\Delta Y}{Y}$$

where Q   is the initial, planned, quantity demanded
Y   is the initial, expected, income
Δ   (the Greek letter delta) denotes a change in the variable concerned.

The change in income is 20 per cent or 0·2. For product A the change in quantity demanded is 40 per cent or 0·4. Consequently: IED = 0·4 ÷ 0·2 = 2. When, as in this instance, IED exceeds one, we say that the demand for the product is (income) *elastic*.

Working out IED for the other products gives the values shown in the bottom row of the table. The demand for product B expands exactly in line with income: IED = 1. Demand has *unitary (or unit) elasticity* with respect to income.

The quantity demanded for product C increases, but by less than income: IED = 0·5. Demand for this product is (income) *inelastic*.

For all three products A, B and C, the quantity demanded increases as income increases. All three are *normal goods*.

For product E, on the other hand, demand falls; IED = −0·5. Product E is an *inferior good*.

Product D is on the boundary between a normal and an inferior good. IED = 0; demand is *perfectly inelastic* with respect to income.

Qu.4.4   Explain the following: (*a*) budget constraint, (*b*) inferior goods, (*c*) complementary products.

Necessities and luxuries
It is possible to make some broad generalisations about the IED of various product groups. What we often call the necessities of life – food, shelter, fuel – tend to have a low IED. Indeed, as we have seen, some basic food items have a negative IED; they are inferior goods. On the other hand, so-called luxury products – consumer durables, foreign holidays, etc. – tend to have a high IED.

However, it must be remembered that these are broad generalisations, to which many exceptions can be found. For example, in countries which have experienced famine, basic foodstuffs have a very high IED. For many people in these countries virtually all of any increase in income would be spent on food.

Let us take personal transport as another example. At an early stage of a country's economic development, the only form of mechanised personal transport that most people can afford is a bicycle. Consequently at this stage IED for bicycles is high. Subsequently, as incomes continue to rise, many people are able to purchase motor-cycles and cars, and fewer people purchase bicycles. The IED for bicycles falls and eventually becomes negative; it has changed from being a normal to an inferior good. (It can be seen that the term inferior does *not* refer to the *quality* of the product.)

> **Qu. 4.5** Choose two products for which you think income elasticity of demand is likely to be (*a*) high, (*b*) low, over the next ten years. Explain your choice.
>
> **Qu. 4.6** 'Once an inferior good, always an inferior good.' Discuss.

Changes in tastes

It is clear that changes in tastes can affect demand. For example, a fashion for shorter skirts causes the demand for cloth, and hence for wool, to fall; the trend towards 'healthy living' leads to a higher demand for brown flour and a lower demand for sugar.

Changes in tastes may occur for various reasons, including a desire for variety, the influence of friends, and information obtained from advertising. When we consider weekly expenditure plans, changes in tastes are usually incorporated in the consumers' initial plans. If Mrs Brown decides that she wishes to lose weight, she will plan to buy less sugar. When longer-term plans are concerned, changes in tastes may cause the initial plans to be revised. For example, a pleasant evening at a barbeque party might cause Mr Brown to buy a barbeque set instead of the exercise bicycle for which he had been saving.

Demand curves: summary

A demand curve relates the quantity of a product demanded to its price. Consumers make expenditure plans which take into account all the *information* that they have and their *expectations* at that time. If, by the time they get to the shops (or wherever they spend their money), they have received no more information and their expectations are fulfilled, they will implement their initial spending plans, i.e. their initial demand curves are unchanged.

On the other hand, if they receive more information or if their expectations are not fulfilled, their demand curves will shift. Their actual expenditure will differ from their planned expenditure. In other words, as time goes on, consumers *learn*, and this learning affects their behaviour.

An alternative view

It is not uncommon to find demand curves interpreted in a slightly different way from that presented here. The initial demand curve (e.g. D_1 in Figure 4.2) refers to the quantities that would be bought at various prices in one period and the new demand curve (D_2) to the quantities that would be bought in a later period. Consumers are assumed to have perfect information in both periods, and the shift in the demand curve is due to a change in circumstances, e.g. in income.

> **Qu. 4.7** Explain the relationship between information and demand.

Market demand curves

A market demand curve is the aggregate of all the individual demand curves for a product. Many products are purchased by thousands or even millions of consumers. Since we cannot illustrate this situation graphically, we take a product for which we assume there are only three potential purchasers, Lord Archer, Mr Black and Mrs Cookson, whose respective demands are indicated in Figure 4.6 by D_A, D_B, and D_C.

It can be seen that Lord Archer has the highest demand. Indeed, at any price within the range $P_1 - P_2$ he is the only purchaser. Within this range his demand curve, D_A, and the market demand curve, D_M, coincide. Once price drops below P_2, Mr Black enters the market; the demand curve is now found by aggregating (horizontally) D_A and D_B. Finally, once the price falls below P_3, Mrs Cookson also enters the market; the demand curve is the aggregate of D_A, D_B, and D_C.

The three individual demand curves are assumed to be independent of each other. This is usually the case in markets for consumer goods, but occasional exceptions may be found. For example, one of the reasons why Lord Archer is prepared to pay a high price for the product may be its exclusivity. If so, he may buy *less* of the

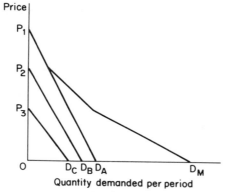

Fig. 4.6 Individual and market demand curves

product when its price falls so low that other people can buy it. In this instance the demand curves would *not* be independent.

The shape of market demand curves

Since individual demand curves usually slope down from left to right, most market demand curves also do so, as shown in Figure 4.6. But certain exceptions to this rule may be found.

Perverse demand curves

Figure 4.7 shows a demand curve which has the usual shape for prices above P, but the reverse shape for prices below P.

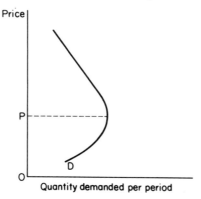

Fig. 4.7 Perverse demand curve

Two main factors account for this backward-sloping or 'perverse' segment of the curve:

1   *Conspicuous consumption*   As noted above, some products may be bought for the purpose of conspicuous consumption ('snob value'). For example, although diamonds are objects of beauty, some of their value derives from the fact that they are known to be expensive. They are a symbol of material success. If the price fell to the level at which everyone could afford them, this motive for purchasing diamonds would no longer exist (although diamonds would still be bought for other reasons). Figure 4.7 shows that below price P, the net result would be a reduction in the quantity bought. In fact producers of diamonds are well aware of this danger and take steps to maintain a high price.

2   *Price as an indicator of quality*   For some products it is possible to judge quality by examination (e.g. fruit and vegetables). But this is more difficult for other products (e.g. carpets). For these products, consumers may take price as an indicator of quality. Less may be sold at a lower than a higher price because consumers see the low price as indicating lower quality.

Price trends

A change in price may be seen by consumers as heralding future price changes; a fall in price as heralding further falls, a rise as heralding further rises. In these circumstances more may be bought at a higher than a lower price. However, this cannot be illustrated on a diagram such as Figure 4.7, since a demand curve refers to the quantities that would be bought at various prices in a *given time period*.

> **Qu. 4.8**   Under what circumstances might a higher price be associated with a greater quantity demanded?

Demand by producers

Producers purchase materials, components, etc., which they convert into the products demanded by consumers. Many of the factors that apply to household or consumer demand apply also to the demand for goods and services by producers, and we briefly review these factors below. (Producers' demand for labour is discussed at length in Chapter 10.)

Planning

Producers plan their expenditure on various products over different time periods. The building and equipping of a new factory may be planned several years before building begins. Expenditure on materials may be planned on an annual basis, with more detailed plans on a shorter-term basis.

There are many reasons why plans may be revised. Most importantly, the demand for the firm's products may suddenly change, causing a change in the firm's requirements for materials and equipment. The firm's income (profit) may turn out to be different from what was expected. If profits are less than expected, the firm may delay or even cancel the purchase of equipment and keep its existing equipment longer than intended.

Substitution

In its search for value for money, the firm will be alive to changes in the relative prices of materials. For example, for some purposes copper and aluminium are substitutes, and if the firm finds that copper is cheaper than expected it may buy more copper and less aluminium than originally intended. However, on the whole there is less opportunity for substitution in industrial than in consumer markets, since the equipment and materials are usually 'engineered into' the goods produced by the firm. The greater the time period, the more opportunities there are to re-design products and therefore to change the materials, etc, used in making those products.

Qu. 4.9 What factors might cause expenditure plans to be revised?

5

Supply

We noted in the previous chapter that producers convert inputs – materials, components, etc. – into products which are required by consumers. In other words, supply is a *response to demand*. In this chapter we analyse the nature of this response.

It must be emphasised that producers seldom have full or perfect information about demand, for two reasons. First, they are unsure about the market demand. The pattern of demand frequently changes, and producers may believe, on the basis of past experience, that at a price of P (Figure 5.1) they might sell anything between Q_1 (demand D_1) and Q_2 (demand D_2).

Second, each individual producer faces further uncertainty because he does not know how consumers will allocate their custom among the various suppliers. Although past experience may again provide a guide, circumstances might have changed. For example, a

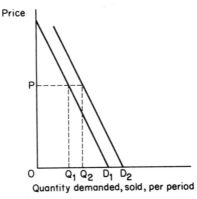

Fig. 5.1   Alternative demand curve

new supplier might have entered the market, or an existing supplier might have changed his price.

Choice of market

We saw in Chapter 1 that one of the major decisions facing producers is which goods and services to produce, i.e. which markets to supply. One of the most important influences on this choice is prospective profitability in the various markets.

The nature of profit

A firm's owners are interested in the rate of return on the money invested in the firm. In order to simplify the analysis we shall assume that the firm has a given, unchanging, capital employed. Consequently a change in total or absolute profits will be reflected in a change in the return on capital employed. For example, if capital employed is £1 million, an increase in profits from £100 000 to £200 000 would represent an increase in the return on capital employed from 10 to 20 per cent.

> **Qu. 5.1** Give an arithmetic example to explain the relationships between the profit margin, total profits, capital employed and the rate of return.

Market supply curves

Once firms have decided which markets to supply, they have to decide how much of the product to supply. A supply curve shows the quantities of a product that would be supplied at various prices in a given period. In Figure 5.2 Q_1 would be supplied at price P_1, Q_2 at price P_2.

Costs and the supply curve

In deciding how much to supply at a given price, the producers take account of the costs of production. Their objective is to cover the costs of production and earn a profit. Consequently, in order to explain the shape of supply curves we must explain how the cost of production changes as output changes.

Output and costs

Average cost is defined as total cost divided by the number of units produced (the quantity of output). As output changes average cost may either remain constant, fall, or rise.

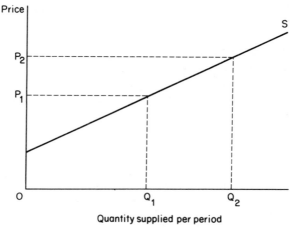

Fig. 5.2　A supply curve

Constant average cost

Figure 5.3 illustrates a very common situation. As output increases, certain fixed costs (e.g. the rates paid on premises, salaries of senior personnel) are spread over more units of output, and this leads to a fall in average cost (cost per unit) up to output Q_1. Beyond output Q_1 average cost is roughly constant, as the fall in average fixed costs is balanced by a rise in other costs (e.g. labour costs per unit of output may rise because of overtime payments). Since the firm

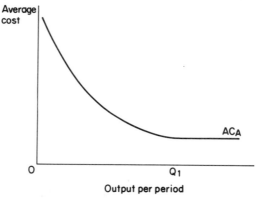

Fig. 5.3　Constant average cost

would expect to produce at least Q_1, average cost is *constant* over the *expected range of output.*

Falling average cost
In Figure 5.4 *average cost continues to fall* as output increases. This is most likely to occur when the time period is sufficiently long to enable the firm to move to a larger scale of organisation, and hence to take advantage of *economies of scale*. Economies of scale are discussed in detail in Chapter 8. They include technical, purchasing, marketing and managerial or administrative economies.

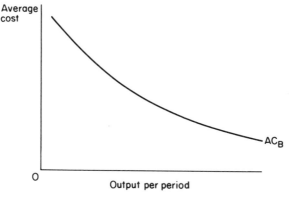

Fig. 5.4   Falling average cost

Rising average cost
Finally, Figure 5.5 shows that *average cost rises* over the range of expected output $Q_1 - Q_2$. Average cost is most likely to rise when there is insufficient time to vary the mix of resources used by the firm. For example, if there is insufficient time to hire and train more workers, it may be necessary for the existing workers to work large amounts of overtime at higher wage rates. If there is insufficient time to purchase new machines, it may be necessary to operate the existing machines at faster speeds than normal, causing higher scrap and reject rates.

Costs, profits and the supply curve

As indicated above, profit constitutes the link between costs and the supply curve. Let us assume that the three producers represented in Figures 5.3, 5.4 and 5.5 are typical of all producers in their markets.

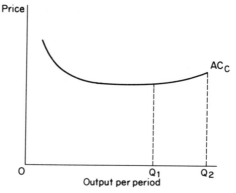

Fig. 5.5   Rising average cost

In other words, over the expected ranges of output, all producers have constant average costs in market A (Figure 5.3), falling average costs in market B (Figure 5.4) and rising average costs in market C (Figure 5.5).

We also assume for the moment that producers require the same profit per unit of output whatever the level of output. The supply curves over the expected range of output will be as shown in Figure 5.6. S_A refers to market A, S_B to market B, and S_C to market C.

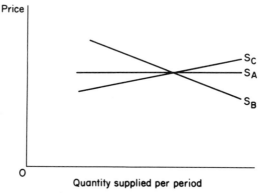

Fig. 5.6   Alternative supply curves

Constant profit margins

How realistic is the assumption that the profit margin is constant at all levels of output? It is realistic in the following circumstances:

(a) Producers aim at a reasonable or fair rate of return, and the profit margin enables them to achieve their objective. They might be able to take advantage of an increase in demand to increase their profit margins but prefer not to do so.

(b) Producers might *wish* to take advantage of an increase in demand to increase their profit margins but do not feel able to do so. Each producer fears that if he were to increase his profit margin he would be undercut by other producers content to accept lower margins. He would lose customers to these competitors and, although his profit margin would be higher, his total profits, and hence his rate of return, would fall because of the loss of sales.

Variable profit margins

Profit margins are most likely to rise when output increases in response to an increase in demand, in the following circumstances:

(a) At low levels of demand and output, producers feel obliged to accept inadequate profit margins. As demand increases they feel able to increase their profit margins to a more acceptable level.

(b) Following from the previous point, each producer believes that at high levels of demand there is little or no danger of being undercut, since all producers are seeking to widen their profit margins.

Costs, profit margins, and the supply curve: summary

The discussion in the previous sections is summarised in the table below. Six possible situations are considered as output rises in response to an increase in demand, and the shape of the supply curve in each situation is identified.

Alternative Supply Curves

As output rises: Average cost	Profit margin		Supply curve (left to right)
1 is constant	(a)	is constant	is horizontal
	(b)	is variable	slopes up
2 falls	(a)	is constant	slopes down
	(b)	is variable	not known
3 rises	(a)	is constant	slopes up
	(b)	is variable	slopes up

Constant average cost may be associated with either a horizontal (1a) or an upward-sloping (1b) supply curve. Falling average cost is associated with a downward-sloping supply curve if the profit margin is constant (2*a*). But if the profit margin is variable (2*b*) we cannot predict the slope of the supply curve. The fall in cost may outweigh, balance or be outweighed by the increase in the profit margin as output increases. Finally, rising average cost is associated with an upward-sloping supply curve (3*a*, 3*b*).

Qu. 5.2 Under what circumstances is the supply curve likely to (*a*) slope up from left to right, (*b*) slope down from left to right, (*c*) be roughly constant?

Time and the supply curve

We have seen that the behaviour of costs as output changes, and hence the shape of the supply curve, is likely to be affected by the time period under consideration. The shorter the time period, the more likely it is that the time period will be so short that the supply curve is vertical.

Vertical supply curve

In Figure 5.7 the vertical supply curve indicates that the same amount, Q, would be supplied whatever the price, i.e. supply is perfectly inelastic with respect to price. Such a situation occurs when a given amount of a product, usually an agricultural product, is brought to an auction market. Having brought the product, the suppliers have to accept whatever price is offered (see Chapter 6). The supply curve would also be vertical if it was impossible to increase the quantity of a vital factor of production (e.g. skilled labour) in the time period under consideration.

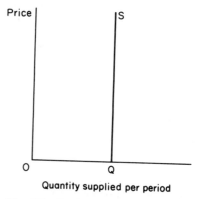

Fig. 5.7 Perfectly inelastic supply

In other instances the supply may be restricted in order to obtain as high a price as possible. However, such a policy will be adopted only if:

(*a*)   the entire supply is in the hands of a single producer, or
(*b*)   all the producers agree that supply should be restricted.

These conditions are seldom found in practice.

> **Qu. 5.3**   Discuss the influence of time on the shape of supply curves.
>
> **Qu. 5.4**   'It is always possible to squeeze a little more output out of the workforce. Consequently supply curves cannot be vertical.' Discuss.

Other influences on supply

So far in this chapter we have been concerned with the relationship between price and the quantity supplied, a relationship encompassed in the *shape* of the supply curve. There are many other influences on supply, and these influences affect the *position* of the supply curve. It follows that a change in any of these other influences will cause a *shift* of the supply curve. Supply curves may shift for several reasons:

Change in the costs of production

Costs of production may change because:

1   *The cost of inputs changes*   For example, the firm grants a wage increase, or raw material prices rise or fall.
2   *Productivity changes*   Productivity is the ratio of output to input, and a change may occur in the productivity of a single factor, such as labour. For example, workers may learn by experience to perform tasks more quickly. On the other hand labour productivity may fall because workers restrict their work-rate to try to win concessions from the management.

Productivity of all factors of production taken together ('total factor productivity') may also change. Experience may reveal more efficient working methods, leading to improved use of labour, machines and materials.

It is sometimes possible to balance the effect of higher input costs by increased productivity. In Figure 5.8 a shift of the supply curve from S_1 to S_2 indicates an increase in average cost (due to higher input costs and/or lower productivity). In order to compensate for the higher costs, the firm requires a higher price at any given output. A shift from S_1 to S_3 indicates a fall in average cost (lower input costs and/or higher productivity).

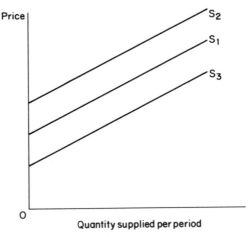

Fig. 5.8   Changes in supply

Qu. 5.5   Draw supply curves to illustrate the following se-
quence of events: (i) A firm grants a wage increase of
5 per cent; then (ii) the firm negotiates an agreement
which leads to an increase in labour productivity of
3 per cent.

Change in profit margins

If firms require (and obtain) a higher profit margin at any given
output, the supply curve will shift up (S_2 in Figure 5.8). This might
occur because the producers become aware of more profitable
alternative uses of resources, and therefore require higher profits if
they are to continue to supply their existing markets. In other
words, the *opportunity cost* of the existing use of resources has
increased.

On the other hand, if alternative uses of resources become less
profitable, firms in this market may have to accept lower profit
margins (S_3). Otherwise new suppliers might enter the market and
undercut them.

Qu. 5.6   Define opportunity cost and show how it can affect
supply.

Expenditure taxes and subsidies

There are two basic forms of expenditure or indirect tax:
(*a*)   A specific tax is levied at a given amount per unit of the

Fig. 5.9   Indirect taxes and supply

product sold (e.g. £1 per gallon of petrol). Customs and excise duties are usually specific. In Figure 5.9 the introduction of a specific tax causes the supply curve to shift from S_1 to S_2. (Note that the two curves are parallel.)

(b) An *ad valorem* tax is levied as a percentage of the selling price. Value added tax is the best known example. In Figure 5.9 the introduction of an *ad valorem* tax causes the supply curve to shift from S_1 to S_3

S_4 in Figure 5.9 illustrates the impact of a specific *subsidy*, i.e. a subsidy of a given amount per unit.

Qu. 5.7 Explain how the supply curve might shift following: (a) an increase in profit margins, (b) an increase in productivity, (c) a fall in the prices of raw materials.

Qu. 5.8 Distinguish between, and give examples of, a specific and an *ad valorem* tax.

Impact of supply on demand

This chapter has considered how supply might change in response to changes in demand. In some circumstances the activities of suppliers have a significant impact on demand.

The most obvious example is where a new or vastly improved product is introduced, e.g. a videophone. Consumers might have some vague idea about the usefulness of such a product, but the formulation of expenditure plans (and thus of the demand curve) would await the product's introduction.

In such situations we can say that supply is a response to expected demand. But it is equally true to say that actual demand is a response to supply. These situations are explored in greater detail in Chapter 9.

> **Qu. 5.9** In what sense, if any, can supply be said to create demand?

6

The Interaction of Demand and Supply

Having discussed in the previous two chapters the factors that influence demand and supply, we now show how these two sets of factors interact. We make extensive use of demand and supply curves. We mainly use downward-sloping demand curves and upward-sloping supply curves, although we make some reference to alternative forms.

Equilibrium price and output

In Figure 6.1, S is the supply curve and D the demand curve for a given product, say beef or aluminium. The curves intersect at X, the point of equilibrium. At this point the plans of purchasers, to buy Q units at price P, coincide with the plans of suppliers, to sell Q units at price P. P is the *equilibrium* or *market-clearing price*, and Q the *equilibrium output*.

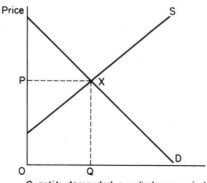

Quantity demanded, supplied, per period

Fig. 6.1   Equilibrium price and output

Note that X is the *only* point of equilibrium. At any price other than P there would be either excess demand or excess supply.

Excess demand

In Figure 6.2 we start from a position of equilibrium. With demand D_1 and supply S, output Q_1 is sold at price P_1. Demand then increases, due perhaps to an increase in income. The demand curve shifts to D_2. If producers, not realising that demand has increased. maintain price P_1, there will be an excess or unsatisfied demand Q_1Q_2, i.e. the situation is one of *disequilibrium*.

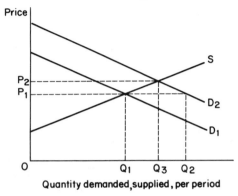

Fig. 6.2   Increase in demand, price and output

The producers will gradually become aware that the situation has changed as the flow of orders increases, as existing customers begin ordering larger quantities and as enquiries are received from new customers. Once they realise that demand has increased, producers raise the price. Equilibrium is eventually restored when price has increased to P_2, at which Q_3 units are sold. (If the supply curve had been horizontal, this would indicate that producers would have maintained price and increased output to meet the increased demand.)

Excess supply

In Figure 6.3 we again start from an equilibrium position in which Q_1 units are sold at price P_1. But in this instance demand falls from D_1 and D_2. If producers maintain price P_1 they will sell only Q_2, whereas they had planned to sell Q_1; i.e. there is an excess supply of Q_2Q_1. This excess supply would manifest itself in unsold stocks. As stocks build up, the producers, realising that demand has fallen,

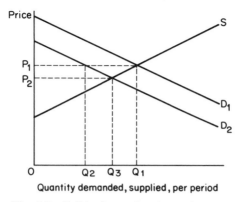

Fig. 6.3 Fall in demand, price and output

revise their plans. Equilibrium is restored when price has fallen to P_2, at which Q_3 units are sold.

Qu. 6.1 Define the terms *equilibrium price and output, excess demand* and *excess supply*.

Other disequilibrium situations
In the situations discussed above, the producers' plans had to be revised because of changes in demand. In a similar way consumers may need to revise their plans because of changes in supply.

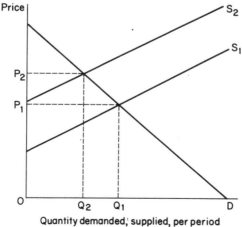

Fig. 6.4 Fall in supply

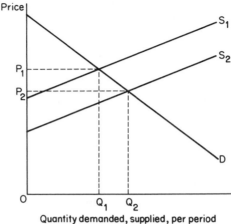

Fig. 6.5   Increase in supply

In Figure 6.4 the initial supply curve is S_1. There is then a change in supply from S_1 to S_2, due, for example, to the imposition of a tax on the product. This leads to an increase in the price from P_1 to P_2, and a fall in the quantity purchased from Q_1 and Q_2.

Conversely, in Figure 6.5 a shift of the supply curve from S_1 to S_2 (caused perhaps by a reduction in the rate of tax or a fall in the cost of production) leads to a fall in price from P_1 to P_2 and an increase in the quantity demanded from Q_1 to Q_2.

Reallocation of resources

In all of the situations considered above, resources are reallocated as a result of a change in either demand or supply. We now examine this process of *resource reallocation* in greater detail, with reference to one of those situations.

Increase in demand

Let us apply the situation illustrated in Figure 6.2 to the market for shoes. The demand for shoes increases and producers respond by increasing output. In order to do this they must employ more resources. They may recruit more labour and run their existing machinery on a two-shift basis. Alternatively they may employ more labour *and* machinery.

The reallocation of resources will end at this point if both of the following conditions are fulfilled:

(*a*) There is sufficient spare capacity in the economy to enable shoe manufacturers to employ more resources without attracting them from other industries. They recruit only workers who were previously unemployed; machinery is bought only from firms whose production capacity would otherwise have remained idle.

(*b*) Increased consumer spending on shoes does not imply less spending on other products. This condition might be fulfilled if the increased spending was financed by an increase in income or by a reduction in saving.

If these two conditions are *not* fulfilled, the increased demand for shoes will affect the allocation of resources in two further ways:

(*a*) If there is insufficient spare capacity to meet the needs of the shoe manufacturers, resources will have to be attracted from other markets or industries. In an attempt to retain resources, other producers will be prepared to pay higher prices for resources (e.g. to increase wage rates). In other words, supply curves in other markets will shift up, as shown in Figure 6.5. Prices in these other markets rise, less is demanded and produced. Resources flow out of these markets.

(*b*) The demand for shoes may increase because of a change in tastes or following an advertising campaign. The extra spending on shoes is financed by lower spending on other products. The situation in these other markets is depicted in Figure 6.3. Following the fall in demand less is produced, i.e. resources are released from these industries.

In the above example, resources were reallocated following a change in demand. In other instances a change in supply may be the starting point of resource reallocation.

Qu. 6.2 Show how a disequilibrium position may arise, and explain why it might not be corrected immediately.

Qu. 6.3 Explain how resources are reallocated through the price mechanism.

Qu. 6.4 Trace the likely effects of an increased demand for motor cycles on the output of (*a*) gearboxes, (*b*) crash helmets, (*c*) bicycles.

Qu. 6.5 Trace the likely effects of an increased supply of oranges on the sales of (*a*) oranges, (*b*) apples, (*c*) orange juice.

The reallocation of resources in response to changes in demand and supply is one of the strengths of the 'free market economy', although this process also has some potential disadvantages. Consequently the allocation of resources is discussed at greater length in the following chapters. To conclude this chapter we show how the response of demand and supply to the change in price can be measured.

Price elasticity of demand

Price elasticity of demand (PED) is defined as the proportionate (or percentage) change in quantity demanded divided by the proportionate (or percentage) change in price.

$$PED = \frac{\Delta Q}{Q} \div \frac{\Delta P}{P}$$

where Q is the quantity demanded of a product
       P is its price
       Δ is a small change in the variable concerned.

The table below shows five possible reactions to an increase in price from 100 to 110 pence, i.e. an increase of 10 per cent. In each instance the quantity demanded at a price of 100 pence was 100 units, and the first row of the table shows the quantity demanded at a price of 110 pence.

Price elasticity of demand

Product	A	B	C	D	E
Quantity demanded	80	90	95	100	105
PED	−2	−1	−0·5	0	+0·5

Applying the formula given above to product A, we have:

$$PED = \frac{-20}{100} \div \frac{10}{100}$$

$$= \frac{-0.2}{0.1} = -2$$

The quantity demanded falls from 100 to 80, i.e. by 0·2 (20 per cent), following an increase in price of 0·1 (10 per cent). When −0·2 is divided by 0·1 the answer, the price elasticity of demand, is −2. The values of PED for the other four products, given in the bottom row of the table, are calculated in the same way.

Classification of price elasticities of demand

Since different products have different PEDs, it is useful to classify these different values. Five classes or categories can be identified, as shown in the following table. The letters in brackets refer to the five products listed in the previous table.

Value of price elasticity of demand	Category
Negative and greater than one (A)	elastic
Negative and equal to one (B)	unitary elasticity
Negative and less than one (C)	inelastic
Zero (D)	perfectly inelastic
Greater than one (E)	positive

As we have shown above, the quantity demanded usually varies inversely with the price, e.g. an increase in price causes the quantity demanded to fall. This happens for three of the products: A, B, and C. For product A the percentage change in quantity demanded is greater than the percentage change in price, so demand is *elastic*; for product B the percentage changes are equal, so demand has *unitary elasticity*; for product C the quantity demanded changes less than price, so demand is inelastic.

If the quantity demanded is unchanged (product D) demand is said to be *perfectly inelastic*. Finally, as we saw in Chapter 4, there may be a few situations in which a higher price is associated with an increase in the quantity demanded (product E). These products have a perverse or backward sloping demand curve, and demand is said to have a *positive elasticity*.

Factors affecting the elasticity of demand

Demand tends to be *inelastic* with respect to price when:

(*a*)   the product is a necessity, or
(*b*)   there are no close substitutes.

The classic example of a product which fulfils these conditions is salt. Its use in cooking is considered essential by many people and no other additive has the same effect on taste and flavour. (Note however that demand for salt supplied by one producer might be highly elastic. There are few differences in the salt supplied by various producers; consequently if one producer were to increase his price he might lose many customers to other producers.)

Demand tends to be *elastic* with respect to price when there are close substitutes for the product. For example, if the price of beef rose, consumers would reallocate some of their spending to other types of meat. If the price of cinema seats rose, people would spend more time at home watching films on television.

Qu. 6.6 Why would you expect the elasticity of demand to be (*a*) lower for fish than for trout; (*b*) lower for all trout than for trout sold by one fishmonger?

Time and elasticity

In general, PED tends to be higher the longer the time period. Given more time, people have more opportunity to search and find substitute products. There is also more opportunity to modify technical conditions. We saw in Chapter 4 that time is especially important for producers, since they may need to redesign products if they wish to substitute one component or material for another. But it can also be important in some purchasing decisions by consumers. For example, if the price of gas falls relative to other fuels such as oil, consumers have a strong incentive to switch to gas from other forms of central heating. However, they need time to convert their appliances or buy new ones. Similarly, when the price of rail fares rise, consumers have an incentive to switch to private transport, but many may not be able to afford to purchase a car or other vehicle immediately.

Qu. 6.7 Outline the factors that influence the value of price elasticity of demand.

The significance of price elasticity of demand

In Figure 6.6 there are two demand curves. D_I is inelastic, and D_E elastic, over the range of prices that we shall discuss. The initial

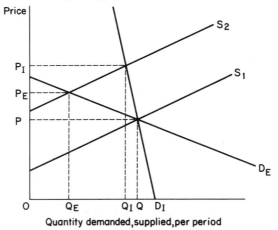

Fig. 6.6 Elastic and inelastic demand

position is one of equilibrium, with Q bought at price P. When the supply curve shifts from S_1 to S_2, the increase in price is much greater with the inelastic than the elastic demand curve, and the fall in quantity demanded is much less.

In order to explain the significance of these differing elasticities, let us consider the various possible causes of the shift of the supply curve.

1 *An increase in input costs* (e.g. higher wage rates) When workers are negotiating higher wage rates, they should take account of the price elasticity of demand for the products that their firm makes. For a given increase in the wage rate (a given shift of the supply curve), the rule is as follows: the more elastic the demand for the firm's product, the greater is the fall in the quantity demanded, in output and in employment.

2 *An increase in profit margins* We have seen that producers are concerned with their total profits. If demand is highly elastic an increase in profit margins may lead, via a substantial fall in the quantity sold, to a fall in total profits. On the other hand, if demand is inelastic there will be only a small fall in the quantity sold and total profits are more likely to rise.

3 *The imposition of an expenditure tax* Governments sometimes tax products in order to discourage consumption. This aim will be best met when demand is elastic. But in other instances taxes are imposed in order to raise revenue for the government. This aim is

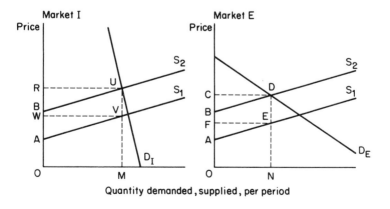

Fig. 6.7 Elasticity of demand and tax revenue

most likely to be fulfilled by taxing products for which demand is inelastic.

This can be seen by comparing the two diagrams in Figure 6.7. The initial supply curves S_1 are identical, as are the initial equilibrium price and output. (To simplify the diagram these points are omitted.) The government then imposes the same rate of tax AB on both products, causing the supply curves to shift to S_2.

The price of product I, for which demand is inelastic, rises to R, at which M is sold. The tax revenue is shown by the rectangle WVUR. (WV is the number of units sold ($= OM$) and VU is the tax per unit ($= AB$).)

The price of product E, for which demand is elastic, rises to C, at which N is sold. The tax revenue is shown by the rectangle FEDC ($FE = ON$; $ED = AB$). It can be seen that far more revenue is raised by the tax on I; the area of the rectangle WVUR is much bigger than the area FEDC.

> **Qu. 6.8** Explain the significance of the price elasticity of demand to (*a*) producers, (*b*) trade unions, (*c*) governments.

Price elasticity of supply

Price elasticity of supply (PES) is defined as the proportionate (or percentage) change in the quantity supplied divided by the proportionate (or percentage) change in price.

$$PES = \frac{\Delta Q}{Q} \div \frac{\Delta P}{P}$$

where Q is the quantity supplied of a product
     P is its price
     Δ is a small change in the variable concerned

We have already seen that an increase in price is often associated with an increase in the quantity supplied, i.e. PES is *positive*. But we have also seen that when demand increases more may be supplied at the existing price, i.e. supply may be *perfectly* or *infinitely elastic* at that price. Finally, when firms take advantage of economies of scale, more may be supplied at lower than at higher prices, i.e. supply has a *negative elasticity*.

Factors influencing elasticity of supply

The main factors influencing the value of the price elasticity of supply are the ease and cost of acquiring additional resources (and of disposing of existing resources when producers wish to reduce the quantity supplied). These are in turn influenced by the length of the time period under consideration. As we saw in Chapter 5, at one extreme the supply curve might be vertical if the time period is very short. At the other extreme the supply curve might slope down when sufficient time elapses for producers to gain economies of scale.

The significance of elasticity of supply

A given change in demand will result in a bigger change in price, the less elastic is supply. In general, supply is less elastic for primary products than for manufactured goods, especially in the short term. Consequently far bigger price fluctuations occur in primary markets.

> **Qu. 6.9**   How would you explain the fact that supply is usually less price elastic for primary products than for manufactured goods?

Factor markets

Having seen how resources are reallocated in product markets, we shall now see how demand and supply interact in the markets for factors of production. The discussion is relatively brief, partly because many of the principles are common to both types of market, and partly because the labour market is discussed in greater detail in Chapter 10.

Demand for factors of production

A factor of production is demanded not for its own sake but because of its value in use, i.e. the demand is a *derived demand*. A businessman will acquire land, purchase and equip buildings, and hire labour in order to produce something. He hopes, of course, that the revenue obtained from the articles he produces will exceed the cost of production.

Demand curves for factors of production

As usual, a demand curve shows the quantities of a factor that would be purchased (in a given period) at alternative prices. Figure 6.8 shows that the quantity demanded is inversely related to the price.

This relationship between price and quantity demanded could have several causes:

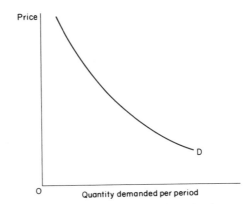

Fig. 6.8 Demand for a factor of production

Substitution
Most products can be produced by alternative combinations of resources and, as noted in Chapter 1, the combination chosen depends upon the factors' relative prices. As the price of one factor rises relative to that of other factors, less of that factor (and more of other factors) will be employed. If wage rates rise, employers instal labour-saving machines, i.e. capital is substituted for labour. (Substitution may not occur immediately, for the reasons outlined earlier.)

Impact in product markets
Even when the process of substitution has been completed, costs of production are likely to be higher than previously. These higher costs will lead to a fall in output. If the firms increase their prices to compensate for the higher costs, the quantity demanded by consumers will fall, causing a fall in the demand for factors of production.

Diminishing productivity
As more units of a factor are employed, each additional unit may be of less value (i.e. add less to output) than the previous unit. Consequently it is worth employing more factors only at a lower price. The fall in productivity could occur for two reasons:

(a) The quantity of at least one other factor is fixed. The example favoured by many textbook writers is the farmer who employs more labour on a farm of a given size. At first productivity may increase, since some jobs can only be undertaken by several men working together. But eventually productivity declines as the additional labour is used to perform less and less essential tasks. (It is possible to envisage a situation in which there are so many workers that they get in each other's way; the employment of more workers could then actually cause output to fall.)

In practice employers wishing to expand output usually increase the quantity of all the factors of production. Consequently our farmer is better seen as an example of what *could* happen rather than what usually happens.

(*b*) Different units of the factor vary in quality (e.g. some people work harder than others, and some plots of land are more fertile than others). At lower prices it becomes profitable to employ lower quality inputs that would not have paid their way at higher prices. (If differences in quality are very marked it may no longer be possible to use a single demand curve.)

Changes in demand

The demand for a factor of production will increase (the demand curve will shift to the right) if demand increases for the goods or services in whose production that factor is used. Conversely, the demand for the factor will fall if the demand for these goods and services falls.

The demand for a factor of production may also change following a change in the price of other factors. However, it is impossible to predict the outcome of these changes. For example, let us consider what might happen to the demand for labour when the price of machines (capital) falls.

On the one hand, the demand for labour will *fall* as firms substitute machines for labour. On the other hand, the fall in the cost of production may lead to a fall in product prices and therefore an increase in quantity demanded. This will lead to an *increase* in the firm's demand for all factors of production, including labour. There is no way of predicting the net effect on the demand for labour of these conflicting tendencies.

> **Qu. 6.10** Explain the term *derived demand* and discuss its significance.

Supply curves

The supply curve in Figure 6.9 shows the quantities of a given factor that would be supplied (in a given period) to a group of firms at alternative prices. All factors have alternative uses, and as the price

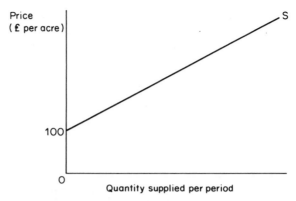

Fig. 6.9   Supply curve for land for factory building

paid in this use increases, more of the factor is attracted away from other uses.

The labour market is discussed in detail in Chapter 10, so we shall consider here an example relating to another factor of production, land. Assume that Figure 6.9 refers to the supply of land for factory building. It can be seen that unless developers pay a price of at least £100 per acre they will not be offered any land. All the land would be used for other purposes (e.g. shops, office blocks). As the developers increase the price they are willing to pay, more land is attracted from these alternative uses and is made available for factory building.

Changes in supply

If a change occurs in potential profitability in alternative uses, the supply curve will shift. For example, if the development of offices became less profitable, more land would be made available for factory building (the supply curve of land for factory building would shift to the right). If office development became more profitable, the supply curve would shift to the left.

Equilibrium in factor markets

Equilibrium has exactly the same meaning in factor as in product markets. Figure 6.10 again relates to land for factory building. With the initial demand curve D_1 and supply curve S_1, Q_1 land is traded (sold or rented) at price P_1. An increase in demand to D_2, due to an expansion of the manufacturing sector, would cause the price of land to rise to P_2, at which Q_2 would be traded. A subsequent fall in

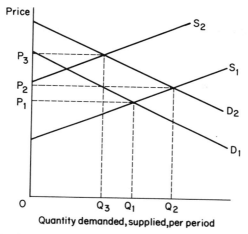

Fig. 6.10   Changing equilibrium in the market for building land

supply to S_2, due to an increase in profitability in alternative uses, would cause a rise in price to P_3 and a fall in quantity traded to Q_3.

7

Alternative Economic Systems

In the previous chapter we showed how resources are allocated via the price mechanism. But this is by no means the only method of allocation, and in this chapter we consider alternative methods.

Classification of economic systems

Economic systems can be defined in terms of three characteristics, as shown in Figure 7.1.

In *free market economies* resources are owned privately and are allocated by the price mechanism. Decision-making is decentralised, decisions such as which goods and services to produce being taken by a large number of 'economic agents' (firms).

In *command or planned economies* resources are owned collectively, by the state, and are allocated by means of a centralised planning process.

In *mixed economies* resources are owned part privately and part collectively, and are allocated partly via the price mechanism and partly by decisions taken centrally by the authorities responsible for planning.

	Free market ----- Mixed -------- Command		
Ownership of resources	Private	Private/collective	Collective
Allocation of resources	Price mechanism	Price mechanism / planning	Planning
Decision - making	De-centralised	Partly de-centralised	Centralised

Fig. 7.1   Alternative economic systems

We now consider the features which *in principle* are found in each of these systems, beginning with a further examination of the free market economy.

Free market economy

As we saw in Chapter 6, in a free market economy resources are allocated via the price mechanism. Consumers purchase goods and services in order to satisfy various wants. These wants constantly change, and this is reflected in a constantly changing pattern of demand. Producers respond to this changing pattern of demand by modifying the mix of goods and services that they supply. This process of supply responding to demand is known as *consumer sovereignty*.

Objectives of producers

Producers respond to consumer demand in order to achieve various objectives – growth, profitability, security, etc. – and they make this response as they wish, i.e. decision-making is de-centralised or dispersed (Figure 7.1).

Competition

In a world of certainty each producer would know which response, which pattern of output, would yield the best 'pay-off', e.g. would lead to the highest profits. But in practice producers are faced with a range of alternative courses of action, the outcome of which is uncertain to a greater or lesser extent. Producers who make the best choices succeed: sales and profitability increase. Producers who make poorer choices fail: sales and profitability decline, and the producer may even go out of business.

Although this competitive process can be very uncomfortable for the less successful firms, it is seen as one of the strengths of the free market system. As less successful firms decline, they release resources which are absorbed by the more successful firms.

Entrepreneurial activity

The term 'entrepreneur' may conjure up a picture of a 'smart operator' sitting behind a large desk, using the telephone to put together a series of lucrative financial deals. The reality is more prosaic than this. Entrepreneurial activity involves combining re-sources in ways which satisfy consumers' wants and producers' objectives. To do this successfully requires a great deal of fairly routine work in market research, production scheduling, quality control and so on.

However, the picture of the smart operator does have something to say about another aspect of entrepreneurial activity. The entrepreneur *searches* for ways of using resources that have not hitherto been recognised. This *alertness* to new opportunities may manifest itself in:

(*a*)   the introduction of new products;
(*b*)   finding new markets for existing products;
(*c*)   using more efficient methods of production.

The free market economy, with its emphasis on decentralised decision-making, is said to foster the entrepreneurial spirit.

> **Qu. 7.1**   Explain the following terms:
> (*a*) consumer sovereignty, (*b*) entrepreneurial activity.

Disadvantages of a free market system

The advantages noted above may not always apply and a free market system may in practice have a number of disadvantages:

(*a*)   Since effective demand depends upon ability to pay, some people may live in great affluence while others live in extreme poverty.
(*b*)   The market mechanism cannot ensure an adequate supply of communal goods such as roads, hospitals and educational facilities. J. K. Galbraith has drawn attention to the existence in the USA of 'private affluence and public squalor'.
(*c*)   *External costs* may arise (e.g. pollution, congestion, noise) which are detrimental to consumers. (External costs are discussed in Chapter 9.)
(*d*)   Consumer sovereignty may be impaired if producers mould consumer demand by advertising and other forms of promotional activity.
(*e*)   Resources, including labour, may remain unused.

Command economy

In a command or planned economy resources are allocated by means of a centralised planning process. The planning authority decides how much of each commodity should be produced in the coming year and allocates production quotas to each enterprise that is authorised to produce the commodity in question. The price at which each commodity is to be sold is also determined centrally.

In order to try to ensure that the final output is produced according to plan, a series of subsidiary plans is drawn up, covering the supply of raw materials, components and equipment. Manpower plans are also made, to avoid output plans being foiled by labour shortages.

The primary objective of every enterprise is to meet its production quota. Consequently most of management's time is taken with ensuring that supplies of materials, etc., arrive on time, and with scheduling output.

Advantages of a command economy

The main advantage claimed for a command economy is that planning ensures that every person's material needs are met, rather than this depending upon the person's ability to pay. Whether the needs are private (e.g. food and shelter) or communal (e.g. roads and defence), the planning authority can allocate the resources required to meet those needs.

Another advantage is that manpower planning can ensure that every person of working age has a job.

Finally, too much competition is believed to be undesirable; it is said that in the command economy, instead of unrestricted competition between one firm and another, between one worker and another, and between one consumer and another, planning ensures cooperation.

Disadvantages of a command economy

The advantages of the command economy discussed above may not always operate in practice. Moreover these economies can have a number of disadvantages:

(*a*) The pattern of output reflects the value systems of the planners, and this may not coincide with that of consumers.
(*b*) This difference sometimes manifests itself in an excess supply of products; in 1984 the Soviet Union, with a population of 275 million, produced 740 million pairs of shoes – more than the combined output of the USA, Great Britain, France and West Germany. Many of these shoes remained unsold, since many people preferred to buy sports shoes and sandals.
(*c*) In other instances supply is inadequate to meet demand, especially for those products whose price is subsidised. For example, in the Soviet Union the official price of meat set in 1962 was not changed for more than twenty years, despite subsequent increases in the cost of production. By 1986 the

price was only 40 per cent of the cost of production. The low price meant that demand outstripped supply, and the state butchers' shops frequently had large queues of customers.

(d)   Since profit is not a measure of an enterprise's performance, there is little incentive to increase efficiency (e.g. by raising productivity). Indeed, enterprises may prefer to operate with a certain level of inefficiency, as a 'reserve' to be used if their production targets are raised.

(e)   More generally, the search for new ways of using resources is inhibited, since such activity is not rewarded.

(f)   There may be a considerable amount of 'hidden' unemployment, with people being retained in jobs of little economic merit, because they are part of the enterprise's labour quota. In the Soviet Union an enterprise can dismiss workers, but only if it can persuade another enterprise to take them on.

(g)   The centralisation of economic power makes it easier for the state to exercise political power and to curtail the freedom of individuals.

> **Qu. 7.2** What are claimed to be the main advantages of (a) a free market economy, (b) a command economy?
>
> **Qu. 7.3** What are the main disadvantages of (a) a free market economy, (b) a command economy?

Modifications to the command economy

Political changes in the 1980s led to modifications in the Soviet and Chinese economic systems that took them slightly further from the command end of the spectrum. In 1986 four important reforms were announced in the USSR:

(a)   Collective farms were given the right to sell 30 per cent of their fruit and vegetables through peasant markets rather than through state shops. The higher prices obtainable in these markets would provide an incentive to increase output and to improve the quality of the produce.

(b)   Twenty-nine different types of private enterprise were legalised, including taxi-driving, house and car repair, tailoring and furniture making. People undertaking private activities are not allowed to employ others and they must themselves continue to hold a state job, although this is often nominal in practice. This measure was expected to increase the contribution of private labour from 2 to 4 per cent of the national income.

(c)   Private individuals were permitted to establish co-operatives to produce goods. It was estimated that such organisations, previously illegal, should account for between 10 and 12 per cent of national income within ten years.

(*d*) From 1987 the Ministry of Foreign Trade's monopoly over 'hard-currency' exports and imports was broken up. Individual ministries and even some enterprises were allowed to trade directly with foreign companies.

> **Qu. 7.4** What do you think were the main reasons for the economic reforms announced in the USSR in 1986?

Mixed economies

It is possible to identify economies at, or very close to, the two ends of the spectrum shown in Figure 7.1. The USSR and China, despite recent changes, still retain many of the characteristics of command economies. Hong Kong and Singapore are good examples of the free market economy. But in practice most economies are mixed, having features of command and free market economies.

Examples of mixed economies include the USA, Japan, West Germany, France and the United Kingdom (the UK being roughly in the middle of the spectrum).

8

Firms and Industries

In this chapter we discuss the various forms of business organisation ('firms' for short) found in mixed economies. Most of our illustrations are drawn from the UK which, as noted in the previous chapter, is a good example of this type of economic system. We examine the advantages and disadvantages of various types of firm. Finally we look briefly at changes in industrial structure.

Private and public sectors

The first broad distinction to be made is between private and public sector organisations. *Private sector business organisations* are owned by individuals (or by other private sector organisations, such as insurance companies, acting on behalf of individuals). *Public sector business organisations* are owned by the state or an organ of the state. While both forms of organisation are found in a mixed economy, private sector organisations are characteristic of a free market economy and public sector organisations of a command economy, as we saw in the previous chapter.

Private sector business organisations

A useful way of looking at private sector organisations is by considering various stages of a firm's growth.

Sole traders

Most businesses start when someone has a bright idea which he or she wishes to exploit. If the person decides to 'go it alone', he acts as a sole trader. There are a large number of sole traders engaged in a wide variety of trades: plumbing, window-cleaning, retailing, etc.

Sole traders have the advantage of being in full charge of their businesses. On the other hand, they suffer two disadvantages:

(*a*) Their resources are limited to what the owner can provide (plus any borrowing).

(*b*) Sole proprietors have *unlimited liability*; if the business runs into financial difficulties the owner can be obliged to sell his personal assets (e.g. house and car) to meet debts incurred by the business.

The first disadvantage can be overcome by forming a partnership.

Partnerships

A partnership is an association of two or more persons 'carrying on a business in common with a view to profit' (Partnership Act 1890). The number of partners can be as many as twenty (or more for some professions), which means that partnerships have better access to finance than sole traders. (The financing of businesses is discussed in more detail in Chapter 11.)

However, most partnerships still suffer the second disadvantage noted above, unlimited liability. Partners usually share equally in profits and in meeting (from their personal resources if necessary) any debts. Partnerships which are *limited* (see below) are uncommon, and where they exist at least one partner must accept unlimited liability.

Companies

Companies are owned by shareholders. But in law companies are distinct from their shareholders, whose liability is *limited* to the paid-up value of their shares. There are two main types of company:

1 *Private limited companies* Private limited companies, which can be identified by the affix 'Ltd' after their name, are a very common form of business. The number of shareholders is not limited by law, and there are some extremely large private companies (e.g. Littlewoods, the retailer and football pools promoter; Heron International, which has interests in property, car retailing, etc.).

However, private companies are not allowed to make an issue of shares to the general public, and this limits the company's access to finance and, sometimes, its rate of growth. This disadvantage does not apply to the public limited company.

2 *Public limited companies* Public limited companies can be identified by their use of the affix 'Plc' (sometimes written PLC or plc). They are able to issue shares to the general public, and large public limited companies such as Shell, ICI and Marks and Spencer have hundreds of thousands of shareholders. Consequently, although there are far fewer public than private companies (around

10 000 public as compared to three quarters of a million private in the UK), overall public companies control more assets than private companies.

> **Qu. 8.1** List the advantages and disadvantages of each of the following: (*a*) sole traders, (*b*) private limited companies, (*c*) public limited companies.

Multinational companies

Multinational companies (also known as transnational corporations) own or control assets, such as factories or plantations, in two or more countries. Their output is also invariably sold in more than one country. The growing importance of multinationals is due to several factors:

1 The desire of producers to control assets which are used at various stages of the productive process and which are found in different countries (e.g. rubber plantations in Malaysia and rubber factories in Europe).

2 A desire to minimise costs by using cheap sources of inputs. In recent years many multinationals based in Europe and the USA have transferred some production processes to Asian countries such as Taiwan, to take advantage of lower wage rates. The processes which are transferred often, but not always, involve relatively routine operations.

3 As the market in the parent country becomes *saturated*, attention is given to overseas markets. The usual procedure is that these markets are initially supplied from the parent country, i.e. by *exports*. Some producers do not go beyond this stage, but others move to the next stage, establishing local production units in at least some of their overseas markets.

Establishing production units overseas can have several advantages. It can lead to:

(*a*) Reduced transport costs, especially if materials and components can be obtained locally.

(*b*) Improved knowledge about conditions in these markets and help the producer to adapt to those conditions. For example, some changes in design may be required because of differences in climate.

(*c*) Better relationships with governments of these countries; by establishing production units, jobs are created to the benefit of the countries concerned.

> **Qu. 8.2** How do you explain the increasing importance of multinational companies?

Public sector business organisations

Before describing public sector business organisations, let us first consider why they might be established. In a command economy the motive is primarily *political* (although the politicians may attempt an economic justification). Political considerations may also be important in a mixed economy, as illustrated by the debate on nationalisation and privatisation between the Labour and Conservative parties in the UK. But in mixed economies there is a more important *economic* dimension to the debate, and we shall confine our attention to the economic issues.

Economic justification for public ownership

If governments take assets into public ownership, this implies that they believe that private ownership has disadvantages. To illustrate these disadvantages we turn again to demand and supply curves. Figure 8.1, which reproduces an earlier diagram, shows the outcome of the free market process. Given demand D and supply S, the equilibrium price is P, and the equilibrium output Q.

The basic economic justification for public ownership would be that the free market price was too high and quantity sold too low. (It is important to remember that an undesirable price/output combination does not necessarily lead to public ownership. Alternatives that we discuss later include legislation to counter monopolies and restrictive practices, and subsidising private producers. But public ownership may sometimes be the most appropriate remedy.) Given

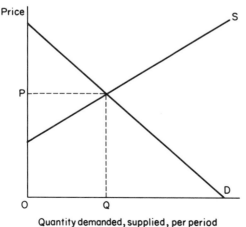

Fig. 8.1   Equilibrium price and output

the demand, a reduction in price and an increase in the quantity sold can occur only if supply changes.

Change in supply
In Figure 8.2 the shift in the supply curve from S_1 to S_2 results in a fall in price from P_1 to P_2 and an increase in the quantity sold from Q_1 to Q_2.

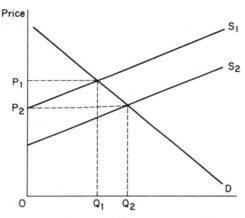

Fig. 8.2   Change in supply, equilibrium price and output

This shift in the supply curve can occur for two reasons:

(*a*)   A reduction in profit margins,
(*b*)   An increase in efficiency.

As a *very* broad generalisation, we can say that publicly owned producers break even (i.e. make zero profit), thus fulfilling the first condition. The second condition may also be fulfilled if public ownership leads to concentration of production and hence to economies of scale that would not be available to smaller private sector firms.

However, there is little evidence that in practice public ownership generally leads to increased efficiency. Indeed, on the whole the evidence points in the opposite direction. This means that even if public ownership leads to lower profits, it does not follow that prices will be lower; in fact they may well be higher.

Qu. 8.3   Present and critically examine the economic justification for public sector business organisations.

Forms of public ownership

Public corporations
Public corporations are common in many countries, including the UK. They comprise:

(*a*)   Nationalised industries, e.g. British Rail, the Post Office.
(*b*)   Other public corporations, e.g. the British Broadcasting Corporation.

The public corporation is intended to gain the benefit of being financed by the state without suffering the disadvantages of constant political intervention in commercial decisions. But in practice governments have been unable to resist intervening. Sometimes intervention has been of a very general kind, e.g. laying down principles to be followed in setting prices or in deciding investment programmes. But intervention has frequently been much more detailed, the senior members of public corporations being constantly required to consult members of the government service.

Provision of goods and services by local authorities
Local authorities provide a wide range of goods and services, such as housing, education and leisure services. Some of these are sold at prices which cover their costs, but most are provided free or at subsidised prices. The remainder of the cost is met mainly by:

(*a*)   local taxation (e.g. rates),
(*b*)   central government grants, financed by national taxation.

Provision of goods and services by central government departments
Most central government departments are concerned with administrative rather than commercial matters. For those departments which are concerned with the supply of goods and services, responsibility is mainly confined to planning orders which are met by producers, mainly in the private sector. So the Ministry of Defence spends large amounts of taxpayers' money on a range of equipment and armaments produced by private firms.

National service organisations
These are organisations which do not fit clearly within local or central government. The National Health Service provides a wide range of medical services, including hospitals, clinics and general practitioner services. Some of these services are provided at a zero price and others at subsidised prices.

> **Qu. 8.4**   Describe the various forms of public sector production.

Co-operatives

A co-operative is a firm owned and operated by a voluntary association of persons (or organisations) in order to provide themselves with goods and services or with employment and incomes.

They are found in both the private sector, as in the UK, and in the public sector, as in the Soviet Union. The two basic types are:

(*a*)   consumer co-operatives, e.g. the various retail societies in the UK;

(*b*)   producer co-operatives, a common form of organisation in Yugoslavia.

Membership of *private sector co-operatives* is achieved by the purchase of shares. In general, producer co-operatives are owned and controlled by those who work in them. Any profits that are not required to finance the future activities of the business are distributed to these members, who comprise all or almost all the workforce. The profits of private sector consumer co-operatives are again distributed to the members. Some members are both workers and consumers, but the majority are consumers only.

Scale of firms

The term 'scale' refers to the maximum output that a firm can produce, and this in turn is closely connected with the firm's size, with the quantity of assets that it controls. We have seen that firms wishing to grow often change their form, sole traders and partnerships usually being smaller than private companies, which in turn are usually smaller than public companies.

Economies of scale

As firms grow they are able to take more advantage of economies of scale, and thus achieve lower production costs. The several forms of economy of scale are discussed below.

Technical economies
There are several sources of technical economies:

1   The cost of plant and equipment often rises less than proportionately to its capacity. For example, a 'Jumbo Jet' aircraft can carry twice as many passengers as some smaller aircraft but does not cost twice as much to build or operate. Similarly doubling the power of machines that drive industrial equipment can usually be achieved without doubling the cost.

2 Economies can often be achieved by *linking* on one site two or more production *processes*, e.g. iron furnaces with steel mills. This can lead to savings in fuel and transport costs. It can also reduce the danger of damage to materials in transit. Finally, it increases the scope for recycling waste products; for example, heat generated in one process can be used in another process rather than going to waste. Processes are more easily linked if they are under common ownership; as the *firm* becomes larger, economies arise, even if the scale of the various processes does not change.

Finally, economies can arise through the operation of the 'law of large numbers'. All plant and equipment needs to be taken out of operation from time to time to remedy defects or breakdowns. The more equipment is installed, the smaller the proportion of spares required.

Consider firms operating transport services (e.g. airlines, taxi services, express freight services) where reputation and success depends upon always fulfilling bookings made by customers. A firm with ten vehicles might feel obliged to keep one of them as a spare, since it knows that one or other of its vehicles is likely to break down from time to time. This one spare vehicle represents 10 per cent of the firm's capacity.

It is highly unlikely that a firm with 100 vehicles would find it necessary to keep 10 spares (10 per cent). Experience might show that no more than, say, three vehicles ever break down at the same time, so 3 per cent spare capacity would be sufficient.

Purchasing economies

Large firms are often able to buy materials, components, etc., on better terms than smaller firms, for the following reasons:

1 Large firms buy larger quantities and so are able to take advantage of the quantity discounts that are offered by many suppliers.
2 Large firms can sometimes use their bargaining power, threatening to take their custom elsewhere unless they are granted better terms.

For example, the Monopolies Commission found that the additional discounts obtained by the three largest and most rapidly expanding grocery chains from fifteen major suppliers averaged almost 8 per cent.

Purchasing economies also arise because the cost of the purchasing function increases less than proportionately to the amount (volume or value) purchased. Especially important is the fact that the number of staff in the purchasing department does not increase as quickly as the amount purchased.

Marketing economies

Very similar principles apply to the marketing side of the firm's business. As sales increase, the cost per unit sold falls as better use is made of equipment (e.g. vehicles, warehouses and labour). Large suppliers are sometimes able to sell on better terms than smaller suppliers, especially to large purchasers.

Risk-bearing economies

Large firms often produce a wider range of products than smaller firms. Consequently they are better protected against the consequences of the failure of one product. If demand falls, or costs rise, to the extent that a product becomes unprofitable, the firm whose business is entirely devoted to that product may become insolvent or bankrupt. On the other hand, the large *diversified* firm can meet the losses out of the profits generated by other products.

Risk-bearing economies are most likely to arise when the firm's products are sold in different markets, e.g. to manufacturing industry and to private consumers, or in domestic and overseas markets.

Managerial or administrative economies

There may well be an overlap here with other forms of scale economy. For example, as the level of purchases and sales increase, it becomes necessary and worthwhile to install computer systems to process orders. This could therefore be seen as a technical economy, since the cost of computer systems increases less than proportionately to their capacity, as well as an administrative economy.

The learning effect

As firms gain more experience in the production of particular goods or services, they discover improvements in production methods which allow them to reduce their costs. These improvements may relate to individual tasks or to the way in which various operations are integrated.

This learning or experience effect was first identified in the production of aircraft in the USA in the 1930s. In the Second World War the production of the famous Liberty ships showed a similar effect, the first taking many months to build, and the last being completed within three days. Experience in these and other industries reveals that average cost declines by 20 to 30 per cent each time accumulated production is doubled.

In Figure 8.3, AC_A shows the average cost of producing various quantities in a given period. The existence of economies of scale means that the higher the output the lower the average cost. Moreover, the learning effect means that the higher the output in this period, the lower the cost of producing any given output in the

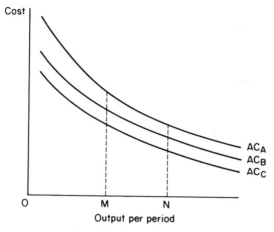

Fig. 8.3 Learning effect

next period. If output in the first period is OM units, the learning effect causes the average cost curve in the next period to fall to AC_B. If output in the first period is ON units, the learning effect is greater, causing the average cost curve in the next period to fall to AC_C.

A virtuous circle

Economies of scale lead to lower production costs. Firms can take advantage of these lower costs in two ways:

(*a*) They can reduce prices, hoping to increase sales and output and thus achieving further economies of scale.
(*b*) They can maintain prices and use the higher profits to finance other activities, such as research into new products.

Limits to economies of scale

At a given point in time there is likely to be an output beyond which no further economies of scale arise. Indeed, if the firm continues to grow beyond this point, *diseconomies of scale* may arise. Limits may arise in relation to each form of economy discussed above:

1 *Technical economies* These may be limited by the nature of materials or by the level of scientific or engineering knowledge. At present, no one has discovered how to build aircraft above a certain size that will actually fly!

2 *Purchasing economies* The cost of inputs may rise if an increase in the firm's requirements causes it to seek supplies from

further afield, or if large-scale purchasing causes prices from existing sources to rise.

3   *Marketing economies*   If an increase in sales requires an extension of the firm's geographical network, this may cause an increase in costs (e.g. because additional warehouses are required or additional transport costs are incurred). Costs may thus rise more than proportionately to output.

4   *Risk-bearing economies*   A point may be reached at which risks have been spread as widely as can be achieved by diversification.

5   *Managerial and administrative economies*   We noted above that large firms can take advantage of elaborate computer systems. But there is some evidence that even these systems may not prevent managerial diseconomies from arising. The larger the firm becomes, the greater is the *potential* for failures in communication and loss of morale leading to absenteeism, high labour turnover and strikes.

Advantages of small firms

Small firms obviously avoid the diseconomies of scale. They may also enjoy some positive advantages:

Rapid response to changes in demand
If the demand for a product changes, the managers or directors of small firms can decide upon their response without having a series of large committee meetings. Speed of response is especially important in markets where fashion plays a big part (e.g. the market for expensive clothes).

Personal service
Personal service may take many forms, including careful attention to detail (e.g. in bespoke tailoring and interior design) and the provision of information; small specialist shops usually provide more information than very large non-specialist shops about the performance and quality of the goods sold.

Finding market niches
Large firms usually prefer to produce large quantities of standardised products; this can leave small but profitable niches in the market that can be exploited by small firms. Small firms have met requirements for unusually high performance (e.g. in sports cars), uncommon sizes (e.g. clothes and shoes), customised versions of goods (e.g. cars), spare parts for old machines, etc.

> **Qu. 8.5**   In view of economies of scale, how do you explain the existence of small firms?

Chain of production and distribution

The chain of production and distribution is far more complex for some products than for others. Consider the two examples in Figure 8.4. The production of screws begins with the extraction of iron ore (other raw materials are ignored here for the sake of simplicity). The iron ore is then smelted and emerges as steel billets (again this is a simplification). The steel billets are then treated in various ways to produce screws. The screws are sold by the manufacturers to wholesalers or other stockists, who repack them in smaller packages and sell them to retail hardware shops. These retailers stock and display these smaller packages for sale to consumers.

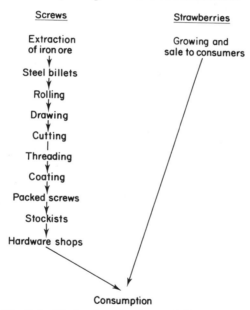

Fig. 8.4   Chain of production and distribution

The series of activities involved may be much simpler, however, as in the case of strawberries being sold fresh to consumers at the farm gate, or even picked by the customers themselves. Here production and retail units are located on the same site and are under common ownership. (By contrast, the activities involved in the production and distribution of screws are probably shared among several firms.) Moreover, there are no manufacturing or wholesaling functions. (Of course, some strawberries may be sold to manufacturers if they are to be used in the manufacture of a different product, such as jam, which will be sold to wholesalers or retailers.)

Qu. 8.6 Explain with examples what is meant by the chain of production and distribution.

Services

The chain of production and distribution for services is obviously different from that for goods. In many instances no extraction of raw materials or manufacturing are involved. However, some service industries involve activities similar to those undertaken by manufacturing firms (e.g. the production of video films for television).

Another difference is that in many service industries, such as hairdressing, the production and the retail functions are undertaken by the same unit. This is uncommon in manufacturing.

In other instances, there is no distribution, as in non-commercial services such as education, and hospital services.

Direction of growth

Firms may grow in several directions, and the terms that are used can be understood by referring again to Figure 8.4.

Horizontal growth (horizontal expansion)
This involves increasing the scale of the firm's existing operations, e.g. extracting more iron ore, rolling more steel, or selling more screws. Horizontal growth is the direction of growth most likely to give rise to technical, purchasing and marketing economies of scale.

Vertical growth (vertical expansion)
This involves a move to an additional stage of production or distribution. If the expansion takes the firm closer to the consumer, e.g. a wholesaler taking over a retailer, it is known as *forward integration*. If it takes the firm closer to the source of raw materials, e.g. a producer of steel beginning to smelt iron ore, it is known as *backward integration*. Vertical growth allows the benefit of linked processes. It may also provide greater security of outlet or supplies.

Diversification
This involves undertaking additional processes or introducing new products that have no or little connection with the firm's existing activities (e.g. a brewery might establish a chain of travel agents). The main motive for diversification is to spread the firm's risks.

Qu. 8.7 Discuss the economies of scale likely to be achieved in each of the following situations: (*a*) a manufacturer of silicon chips increases his market share; (*b*) a clearing bank takes over a firm of estate agents; (*c*) a cinema chain begins to produce films; (*d*) gas showrooms begin to stock electrical appliances.

Forms of growth

Firms may grow by *internal expansion*. Alternatively they may grow externally, by *merger* and *takeover*. The motives for external growth are discussed in greater detail in Chapter 9.

Location decisions

One of the most important decisions taken by firms is where to locate their activities. In some instances the range of options open to the firm is very limited. Ships must be built or assembled close to water and the decision facing the producer is which stretch of river or coast to choose. In other instances there is a much wider choice of technically adequate locations. The ideal site is one that is near to:

(*a*)   sources of all inputs, e.g. raw materials, skilled labour;
(*b*)   all the firm's markets.

In practice few sites are absolutely ideal, and firms often have to compromise. For example, when Nissan opened its first car assembly plant in Europe it chose a site in the North East of England which had numerous advantages, including a large area of flat land, a good supply of trainable labour, and nearness to a port through which components could be imported. On the other hand, the site is not especially well located with respect to Nissan's main markets.

Qu. 8.8 What factors may influence firms' location decisions?

External economies

External economies arise through the *growth of an industry* or a group of firms. As an industry becomes established in an area there develops a network of suppliers of raw materials, services, etc. For example, in areas specialising in metal manufacturing one finds producers of components, heat-treatment plants, and firms able to maintain and repair equipment. The existence of these ancillary industries means that further growth of metal manufacturing in this area is encouraged. In other instances external economies benefit several or even all the industries in the area (e.g. a well developed transport system, local technical colleges).

Qu. 8.9   Explain each of the following terms: (*a*) backward integration, (*b*) diversification, (*c*) external economies.

A classification of industries

Industries can be grouped into three broad categories:

1   *Primary or extractive industries* (e.g. agriculture, fishing, forestry, mining). These industries produce raw materials, most of which are used by the second group of industries.
2   *Secondary industries* (e.g. manufacturing, construction). These industries produce two types of goods: consumption goods, such as cans of peas, refrigerators; and goods used in producing other goods and services, such as drilling machines, computers.
3   *Tertiary industries* (e.g. retailing, cinemas, banking). These industries provide services, either to consumers or to producers.

Changes in industrial structure

As economies develop, primary industries usually become relatively less important. Sometimes this trend is reversed, as when North Sea reserves of oil and gas were developed. But usually the proportion of workers engaged in agriculture, fishing, mining, etc., declines. Conversely, the proportion engaged in manufacturing increases. Subsequently, as the economy continues to develop, growth in the tertiary sector shows the most rapid rate of growth.

These changes in industrial structure reflect the fact that once people have satisfied their need for the necessities of life such as food, shelter and fuel, they spend an increasing proportion of their income on other goods, and subsequently on services.

When one considers an individual country, changes in the structure of industry can occur because of international competition. In the UK employment in manufacturing has declined not only relatively to other industries, but also in absolute terms. The number of employees in manufacturing fell by a quarter between 1977 and 1985. One of the reasons for this is that foreign competitors have taken some of the markets previously supplied by British manufacturers.

Qu. 8.10   How do you account for the changes that have occurred in the relative importance of primary, secondary and tertiary industries?

9

Competition and Monopoly

In earlier chapters we have referred to both the advantages and the disadvantages of the price mechanism. In this chapter we widen our view and consider the advantages and disadvantages of the competitive process, of which the price mechanism is a part.

Forms of competition

A simple definition of competition is 'the process whereby producers seek to increase sales'. In order to increase sales a producer may adopt various forms of competition. For example, he may:

(a) Sell his product (or brand) at a low price relative to the price of other products (or brands).
(b) Offer a product that has features or characteristics not found in other products.
(c) Advertise his products and undertake other forms of sales promotion.
(d) Seek to exercise control or influence over channels of distribution.

A low price

We have already seen that the total amount of a product bought is likely to be greater the lower the price, i.e. market demand curves normally slope down from left to right. The same argument applies to a brand. The lower the price of any brand, relative to other brands, the more will be bought. (This assumes that the consumer does not see the low price as a sign of low quality.) A reduction in the price of Ford cars, for example, would lead to an increase in the number sold (and a reduction in sales of competing models, unless other manufacturers make similar price reductions).

Temporary price reductions

A firm may reduce the price of its products with the intention of driving its competitors out of the market and subsequently raising its price again. Since the price reduction will cause an initial fall in profitability, this can be a dangerous policy and it is most likely to be adopted in one or other of the following circumstances:

(*a*)   A large firm restricts the price reduction to a proportion of its output with the aim of driving out a small competitor, e.g. one supplying a local geographical area.

(*b*)   The price reduction enables the firm to attract the customers of its former competitor(s), and it produces the larger output at a lower average cost. Even if it cannot subsequently raise its price to the original level, it may, because of the reduction in average cost, increase its profits.

Product features

There are innumerable features which a producer can 'build into' a product. The performance, size, styling and colour of goods are likely to be important. Some features are intended to appeal to a wide number of consumers. For example, all purchasers of washing machines are likely to be attracted by superior performance in terms of a cleaner wash, more gentle treatment of the clothes, spinning the clothes drier, and by the greater reliability implied by a longer guarantee period. On the other hand, some features may appeal to a minority but be of no interest to, or may even repel, the majority. For example, a small, fast two-seater sports car may appeal to the rich, young, single businessman but be disregarded by the family motorist, while grandma 'would not be seen dead in it'.

Some large retailers are able to influence the features of the goods they sell. For example, when Marks and Spencer – all of whose goods are sold under their own 'St Michael' label – agree to sell a meat product, they specify the breed of animal, the feed, and the age and the method of slaughter. However, most retailers accept the features as decided upon by the manufacturers. They try to attract custom by offering features relating to the shop (or other form of retail outlet). These features may include a convenient location, convenient opening hours, a wide range of goods, attractive displays, the availability of credit and the provision of before-sales and after-sales service.

Advertising and other forms of sales promotion

Advertising is designed to attract custom by providing information about the existence of products and about their features. This is especially important for new products: however attractive a new product might be, it will not be purchased unless consumers are made aware of it. A good example of *informative advertising* is the announcement in the local paper of entertainments in the coming week.

But advertising often goes beyond the provision of information, being designed to persuade people to buy a certain product or brand. It is sometimes said that *persuasive advertising* works by instilling 'needs' in people, or at least by causing them to recognise previously unrecognised needs.

Many advertisements are a mixture of these two, being designed to present information about a product's features in a persuasive manner. This sometimes involves comparisons with competing brands. For example, a series of television advertisements for a brand of washing powder may show pictures of garments washed with this powder and with a competing 'Brand X' – with, of course, the cleaner wash being claimed to result from the use of the advertised powder.

Qu. 9.1 Give five current examples of advertising that is (*a*) mainly informative, (*b*) mainly persuasive.

Other forms of sales promotion include competitions, trial offers, vouchers to be used for future purchases, and free gifts. We can also include the activities of salesmen and representatives, which are very important for pharmaceutical products, for example. As with advertising, these other forms of sales promotion are partly informative and partly persuasive.

Control of distribution channels

As we explained in Chapter 8, the output of producers is transmitted to consumers via distributors of various types: wholesalers, retailers, etc. If one producer can control these channels of distribution he achieves greater security of outlet for his products. He may also reduce the opportunities of other producers (existing and potential) to bring their products to the attention of consumers.

If a producer owns distributors, he has absolute control over that part of the distribution system. More commonly, producers have sought to exercise control by entering into contracts whereby a distributor agrees to buy a given product from that producer only.

If a producer controls supplies of raw materials, components, etc., he achieves greater security of supply. He may also be able to deny competitors access to supplies, or at least access on terms as favourable as he enjoys.

> **Qu. 9.2** What are the main forms of competition adopted by (*a*) car manufacturers, (*b*) garages which sell cars, (*c*) insurance companies, (*d*) retailers?

The effects of competition

Price competition has been discussed in earlier chapters. Consequently in this section we concentrate on the remaining forms of competition examined above. If a firm succeeds in attracting custom by any of these means, consumers will, of course, have less money to spend on competitive products. This is illustrated in Figure 9.1, which shows the demand for two brands of coffee, X and Y. (To simplify the discussion we assume that only two brands are available.)

In the initial period the demand for each brand is denoted by the demand curve D_1. The producer of brand X then makes a policy change (e.g. implementing a highly effective advertising campaign) which causes demand to increase to D_2. This is accompanied by a fall in the demand for the substitute brand Y to D_2.

It can be seen that the increase in the demand for brand X exceeds the fall in demand for brand Y. This is because the advertising campaign not only persuades some coffee drinkers to switch from brand Y, but also causes people to drink more coffee at the expense of tea.

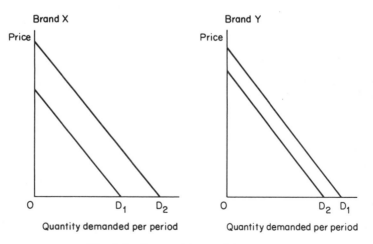

Fig. 9.1   Competition and demand

All successful forms of competition are likely to have these two effects. They cause the total demand for a product to increase, and they cause a change in the market shares of the various brands of that product. Sometimes firms lose so much custom to their more efficient competitors that they make financial losses and withdraw from the market. (This outcome is discussed further below.)

Barriers to new entry

The policies discussed above are often intended both to attract customers from existing competitors and to prevent potential new competitors from entering the market. Potential competitors may also face other barriers to entry, including:

(*a*) High cost of the plant and equipment needed for efficient large-scale production.

(*b*) High cost of advertising on the scale required to achieve a satisfactory volume of sales.

(*c*) Lack of adequate expertise or know-how. Existing firms often acquire, through experience, advantages which it would be difficult for new firms to match.

> **Qu. 9.3** Give examples and explain the significance of barriers to new entry.

Mergers and takeovers

Some of these consequences of competition may also occur as a result of mergers and takeovers. When a merger or takeover takes place, two firms combine to form one. A takeover implies an unwillingness on the part of the firm taken over, while a merger implies agreement between the two firms. However, in a merger there is often a dominant firm which initiates the negotiations, and in this section we use the term merger to include takeovers.

Mergers can take three main forms, each of which has a different purpose:

(*a*) A *horizontal* merger involves two firms at the same stage of production or distribution, e.g. two firms engaged in brewing beer. This form of merger can give rise to several forms of scale economy (see Chapter 8). It also reduces the number of suppliers in the market (see below).

(*b*) A *vertical* merger involves two firms in a buyer-seller relationship. A producer may merge with a distributor in order to obtain greater security of outlet, e.g. a brewery might buy a retail chain of off-licences (an example of *forward integration*). Conversely a producer might merge with a supplier of raw materials, e.g. a brewery with a grower of hops (an example of *backward integration*).

(c)   A *conglomerate* merger involves firms whose activities have no or very little connection. The main purpose is to spread the firm's risks, to avoid having 'too many eggs in one basket'.

Qu. 9.4 What are the main purposes of (*a*) horizontal, (*b*) vertical, (*c*) conglomerate mergers?

Monopoly

Successful competition and mergers can both result in a monopoly situation. In purely theoretical terms, monopoly refers to a situation where there is only one supplier (the monopolist). In countries which have passed laws to control or influence the activities of monopolists, a weaker definition is adopted. For example, in the UK a monopoly situation is said to exist when a supplier accounts for at least one-quarter of the relevant market. (We call such firms *dominant suppliers*.)

Monopoly and economic welfare

Of the various means by which a firm can achieve or maintain a monopoly or dominant position, some would be considered more desirable than others. At one extreme is the firm which supplies at a low price a product with features which appeal to consumers and which are absent from the products of competitors, whose sales suffer as a consequence. At the other extreme is the firm which takes over existing competitors and prevents the emergence of new competitors by controlling supplies of raw materials or distribution channels.

Governments might wish to encourage the first type of behaviour, but discourage the second, and indeed to prevent it by legislation. However, in many countries governments have taken the view that the behaviour of *all* monopolists should be monitored, since monopoly can work against the public interest, even if the monopoly was initially achieved by desirable means. Several possible abuses of a monopoly or dominant position which may give rise to concern, are considered below.

1   *Monopoly profits*   The single-firm monopolist is able to increase its price without losing as many sales as would a firm in a competitive market. It may take advantage of this to earn higher profit margins. This does not necessarily mean that prices will be

higher in monopoly, since the monopolist is likely to enjoy greater economies of scale than would a larger number of suppliers each having a smaller output. Nevertheless, the monopolist could afford to reduce prices and still earn average or normal profit. Earning above-average or super-normal profit is sometimes criticised as benefiting shareholders at the expense of consumers.

2   *Resource allocation*   If prices are higher than required to earn average profit, less of the product will be bought and fewer resources will be employed in supplying that product. The process of free-market resource allocation, discussed in earlier chapters, is impeded.

3   *Restriction of consumer choice*   If the entire output of a product is supplied by one producer, consumer choice is clearly restricted. This is seen as a more serious disadvantage when the monopoly is maintained by 'artificial' or deliberate means (e.g. the control of supplies of raw materials) than by such competitive weapons as supplying a superior product at an attractive price.

4   *Lack of innovation*   If a monopoly is sheltered from competition by artificial barriers it may have less incentive to develop new and improved products, and generally to meet consumers' requirements. (On the other hand monopoly profits may be used to finance research leading to innovation.)

Qu. 9.5 Explain how monopoly might affect economic welfare.

Dominant suppliers

As noted above, in many countries legislation has been introduced to monitor the behaviour not only of single-firm monopolies but also of other dominant suppliers. It is believed that highly concentrated markets, where a large share of total sales is accounted for by a relatively few firms, may give rise to some of the disadvantages associated with the single-firm monopoly. In particular, it is thought that suppliers may be in a better position to reach an agreement to set a price that yields super-normal profits.

Competition and monopoly: summary

Producers use price and various forms of non-price competition in order to increase sales. Successful firms expand their share of the market at the expense of less successful firms; they achieve a dominant, and perhaps even a monopoly, position by satisfying consumers' needs. But a dominant position can also work to the disadvantage of consumers, and in many countries legislation has been introduced to monitor and control the activities of dominant firms. In the United Kingdom the main pieces of legislation are concerned with *collective restrictive practices* and *monopolies and mergers*.

Legislation on collective restrictive practices
Restrictive agreements are agreements, made by two or more firms at the same stage of the productive process, which restrict trade in one way or another. For example, all the manufacturers of a given product might agree to sell the product at a common price. Or all retailers might agree to purchase a product only from a certain group of manufacturers.

The likely effects of such restrictive practices include:

1   *Higher prices* than would occur under free competition. In Figure 9.2 the free market price would be P_1, at which Q_1 would be traded. But producers agree to set price P_2. The consequence of this is that the quantity traded falls to Q_2, implying that fewer resources are required. But when the price agreement is accompanied by a market sharing agreement, all producers remain in business, producing at low levels of output.

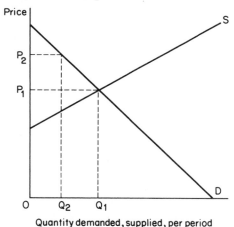

Fig. 9.2   Free market and fixed prices

2   Curbs on competition mean that firms may operate at a *lower level of efficiency*, i.e. a *higher level of cost*, than would be possible with free competition. This is illustrated in Figure 9.3, where the actual supply curve S_2 lies above the potential supply curve

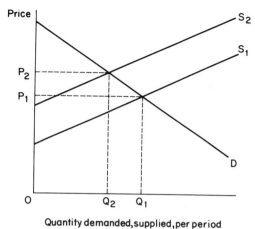

Fig. 9.3 Efficiency and price

S_1. The result is again a higher price and lower level of resource utilisation.

In the United Kingdom collective restrictive agreements can be operated, provided that the Restrictive Practices Court is convinced that the benefits outweigh the disadvantages. In practice it has proved extremely difficult to convince the Court that this is so. Under United States legislation collective restrictive agreements are illegal, whatever their advantages might be.

> **Qu. 9.6** Why have governments in many countries acted against collective restrictive practices?

Legislation relating to mergers and monopolies
In the United Kingdom all proposed mergers and takeovers above a certain size are considered by the government. Those mergers which it is felt might be against the public interest are referred to the *Monopolies Commission* for detailed examination. The Commission balances possible benefits of the merger (e.g. greater economies of scale) against the possible disadvantages (e.g. higher profits, less choice for consumers). It then recommends either that the merger be allowed to proceed or that it be forbidden. The Commission's recommendations are almost always accepted by the government.

The activities of monopolies are also subject to scrutiny by the Commission. If the Commission concludes that the firm has adopted policies detrimental to the public, the government can order the firm to discontinue the offending policies. Government action under this heading has included compelling firms to:

(*a*)   modify their pricing policies, in order to reduce their profits;
(*b*)   abandon price discrimination intended to drive out competitors;
(*c*)   abandon contracts designed to limit customers' freedom to purchase from other suppliers.

Legislation in the UK tends to put fewer curbs on the activities of dominant firms than does legislation in the rest of the EEC and the USA. Moreover, in the USA customers who can prove that they have suffered because of the actions of dominant firms, can claim damages of three times the value of the injury. For example, if a firm had bought a machine for £100 000 when a price of £80 000 would have yielded a normal profit, it could claim damages up to £60 000 (= £20 000 × 3) if the firm was convicted of conspiring with competitors to fix prices.

External costs and benefits

Governments may also intervene in the competitive process because of the existence of *external costs* and *external benefits*.

External costs

We have seen in previous chapters that supply curves reflect the costs incurred by producers in supplying the products in question. We call these *private costs*. The producers hope, of course, to recover these costs from the sale of the products. In other words, private costs affect production and consumption decisions through the price mechanism.

The process of production and distribution may also give rise to costs which do *not* affect production and consumption decisions through the price mechanism. These are known as *external costs*.

As an illustration of the distinction between private and external costs, consider a textile factory which draws water from a river to wash and cleanse fabric, and discharges the waste water, the effluent, into the river. This discharge of effluent pollutes the river and makes it unfit for a range of leisure purposes, such as fishing and swimming.

The private costs incurred by the factory are the costs of installing and operating the machinery which extracts, uses and discharges the water. The external costs comprise the loss of 'consumption' opportunities by anglers, swimmers, etc.

Property rights

The factory is able to use the river for the discharge of effluent for one of two reasons:

(*a*) Property or ownership rights in the river have not been established; to use less technical language, no one knows who owns the river.

(*b*) The owner of the river allows it to be used in this way.

Let us now see what would happen if the owner of the river, realising that he owned a valuable resource, decided to charge the factory for the discharge of effluent. If sophisticated measuring equipment was available, the charge might be related to the amount of effluent discharged, and we can assume that this in turn is related to the factory's output. The effect of the charge in these circumstances is illustrated in Figure 9.4.

The initial supply curve S_1 reflects the factory's costs before the charge is imposed. With demand D, the equilibrium price is P_1, at which Q_1 is sold. A charge equivalent to AB per unit of output is then imposed. The factory wishes to recover this charge through the prices that it sets. The new supply curve is therefore S_2, the new equilibrium price is P_2 and the quantity sold Q_2.

Three things happen as a result of the imposition of the pollution charge:

(*a*) The income of the river owner increases.

(*b*) Consumers buy fewer textiles.

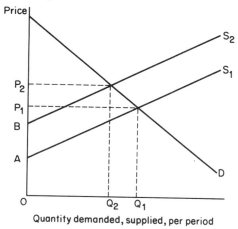

Fig. 9.4 Property rights, price and output

(c)   The opportunities for the 'consumption' of leisure activities (e.g. angling, fishing) may increase, depending upon the extent of the change in pollution. As recent experience in the River Thames shows, once pollution drops below a certain level, fish begin to live and breed. There is also presumably a point below which pollution must fall before swimmers are able to enjoy themselves.

In the above example a producer's activities have a direct impact on the activities of consumers. In other instances a producer's activities have an impact on other producers (and on the consumers of other products).

We can illustrate this by considering a situation similar to that discussed above. Two textile factories are located by a river from which they extract water, and into which they discharge effluent. Factory A is upstream of factory B; consequently its effluent pollutes the water extracted by factory B.

In Figure 9.5 the left-hand diagram relates to factory A. When it is able to discharge effluent without charge, its supply curve is S_1. With demand D the equilibrium price is P_1, at which Q_1 is sold.

The right-hand diagram relates to factory B. B's initial supply curve S_1 reflects the costs incurred in treating the polluted water so that it can be used for, say, washing fabrics. With demand D, price is P_1 and the quantity sold is Q_1.

After a pollution charge is imposed, A's supply curve shifts to S_2, price rises and the quantity sold falls. (This is, of course, the

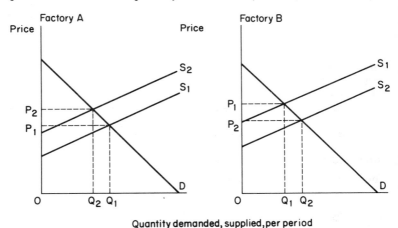

Quantity demanded, supplied, per period

Fig. 9.5   Effects of a charge on pollution

reaction illustrated in Figure 9.4.) The reduction in the level of pollution causes a fall in B's costs, as less time and expense are incurred in treating water. The supply curve shifts to S_2, price falls to P_2 and the quantity sold increases to Q_2.

> **Qu. 9.7** Explain the significance of property or ownership rights.

Methods of reducing external costs

In the above examples external costs were reduced when the owner of the resource (the river) decided to enforce his property rights. Governments can adopt several methods of reducing external costs; these are considered below.

Taxation

If polluters are made to pay a tax which varies with the amount of pollution or the level of output, the effect will be as illustrated in Figures 9.4 and 9.5. However, taxes of this type are costly to administer, and a simpler alternative is a lump-sum tax on all polluters.

Licences

Licensing can be used in two ways:
(a)   To restrict the *number* of producers and hence the level of output and of pollution.
(b)   To ensure that all producers meet *standards*, e.g. do not discharge more than a certain amount of effluent. Firms which do not maintain the specified standards may have their licences withdrawn.

Direct controls

Legislation may be introduced forbidding or limiting pollution. Firms which contravene the legislation may be fined and executives may face imprisonment. Newspapers often carry reports of firms which are fined for polluting, either knowingly or accidentally, rivers or seas, with a consequent death of fish or birds.

Other examples of external costs

There are many other important examples of external costs, some of which we will now consider.

Acid rain

This is the term given to the pollution which results when emissions of sulphur dioxide and other gases react with moisture in the atmosphere to form sulphuric and nitric acids which are subsequently deposited in rain. Among the alleged consequences of acid rain are damage to forests in West Germany and other parts of central Europe; the pollution of lakes in Scandinavia, the UK and Canada, with the destruction of plant and animal life; and the corrosion of buildings, including mediaeval churches and cathedrals in Western Europe.

Acid rain affects consumers in both of the ways noted above: both directly (by reducing opportunities for leisure activities) and indirectly (by increasing the costs of other producers and hence the prices they charge). Considerable attention has therefore been given to the main sources of this pollution – emissions from power stations and car exhausts. The direction of prevailing winds mean that the UK 'exports' a considerable amount of acid rain to other countries, and the UK government has agreed that emissions from power stations will be reduced considerably, although not as much as other countries would wish.

Lead in car exhausts

Lead is added to petrol to increase its octane level and so improve the performance of cars in terms of speed and acceleration. Unfortunately it appears that the lead emitted in car exhausts can be a hazard to health in areas of heavy traffic. Children appear to be particularly at risk, a high lead intake being associated with poor academic achievement and various health problems. Legislation was therefore passed to reduce the amount of lead in petrol. Under EEC law all new cars produced in the Community from 1990 onwards must be able to run on lead-free petrol and, as older cars are scrapped, Europe will gradually become lead-free. Thus external costs will be reduced. But private costs will be increased, if increases occur in the prices of cars and petrol as a direct result of the new requirements.

Noise pollution

In many ways life is becoming noisier, and government action to reduce noise usually takes the form of direct controls. For example, the number of night flights from airports is restricted and local bye-laws prevent the playing of radios late at night or in public places. In factories, firms are obliged by law to protect workers who are subject to high noise levels.

Traffic congestion

Once the flow of traffic on a road reaches a certain level, the progress of other vehicles is impeded. The ultimate in this process is the 'traffic jam' when vehicles make no progress whatsoever. Congestion causes costs of various types, such as heavier petrol consumption and longer journey times, which affect both producers and consumers.

External benefits

Private benefits flow from goods and services that are purchased, i.e. through the price mechanism. But consumers also enjoy benefits that do not accrue via the price mechanism. These are known as *external benefits*.

A simple example is provided by a programme of immunisation against an infectious disease. The people immunised benefit by being protected from disease. But people who are not immunised also benefit: because there are now fewer potential carriers of the disease, the likelihood of their contracting the disease is reduced. If the government believes that freedom from disease is desirable, it may subsidise the programme so that more people are inoculated. (This is in fact an example of a merit good, discussed below.)

In Figure 9.6 the supply curve S_1 reflects the producers' private costs. At P_1, Q_1 people are inoculated. If the government provided a subsidy of P_1P_2 per unit, the price would be reduced to P_2 and Q_2 people would be inoculated. If this was not considered sufficient, the government might increase the subsidy so that inoculations were provided free. The number of people being inoculated would then be Q_3; the only people not inoculated would be those whose fear of inoculation outweighed their estimate of the benefits.

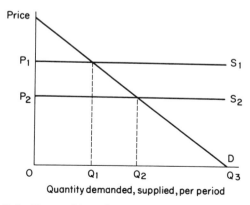

Fig. 9.6 External benefits, subsidy, price and output

Qu. 9.8 Explain why the existence of external costs and benefits may cause governments to intervene in the competitive process.

Qu. 9.9 By what means might governments reduce external costs?

Merit goods

If the government, acting on behalf of society, decides that the free interplay of market forces would result in an inadequate consumption of a good (or service), that good is termed a merit good. The government might consider consumption to be inadequate because of the existence of external benefits, as in the example given above. Or the government might believe that some people who ought to be able to consume the good are not doing so because the price is too high.

As we saw above, the government could reduce the price by giving a subsidy to private sector producers. Alternatively, public sector producers could sell the good at a loss, the deficit being met out of general taxation.

We assumed in the above example that sufficient would be supplied to meet demand, even at zero price. In practice this does not always happen. For example, there are long waiting lists for many operations provided free under the National Health Service in the UK.

Demerit goods

These are goods whose consumption the government wishes to discourage. It can do so either by imposing direct controls (e.g. on cannabis) or by taxation (e.g. cigarettes).

Public goods

The term 'public good' is applied to any product that fulfils two conditions:

(*a*)   If the product is supplied to one member of the community it must be supplied to other members.
(*b*)   If the product is consumed by one person it can still be consumed by others.

Defence is a helpful example of a public good. The fact that my next door neighbour enjoys freedom from attack by enemy troops does not prevent me from enjoying that freedom. (In practice, scarcity of resources may mean that the above conditions are not fulfilled. If missiles are used to destroy enemy missiles aimed at London, those missiles cannot then be used to destroy other missiles aimed at Glasgow.)

The characteristics of public goods mean that responsibility for their production usually lies in the public sector (although, as pointed out earlier with reference to defence, the actual production may be undertaken by the private sector). To understand why this is so, consider the situation which might face a private sector producer contemplating building a barrage to reduce the danger of flooding, such as the barrage built across the River Thames.

The main beneficiaries of this barrage are the people who live or work near to the river, and whose houses and businesses would be affected by flooding. Let us assume that, faced with an estimate of the costs and benefits of the scheme, everyone agreed that the likely benefits outweigh the costs. It may nevertheless be impossible for the producer to raise the necessary finance in advance. Because each person's share of the cost is so small, many people may believe that the scheme will proceed even if they do not themselves contribute, i.e. that they will be able to enjoy the benefits without contributing to the cost. This is known as the *free-rider* problem.

The producer might consider financing the scheme by levying a charge after the scheme's completion. But this would not be practical for a private sector producer, since he could not allow the benefits (freedom from damage by flooding) to be enjoyed by some people while denying them to others.

Consequently the production of public goods is almost always the responsibility of the state. The government is able to finance their production either out of general taxation or by levying a charge which all potential beneficiaries are obliged to pay.

Qu 9.10 Define (*a*) merit goods, (*b*) public goods, and explain their significance for government policy.

10

Labour and Employment

We examined in Chapter 1 some of the factors that influence people's choice of occupation and job. In order to take the analysis further it is useful to make a broad distinction between two types of rewards that work can provide: financial and non-financial rewards.

Financial rewards
The main financial reward from employment is, of course, the workers' wages and salaries. Other financial rewards include employers' pension contributions and various types of bonus, but these are often related to the wage or salary. Consequently we can simplify the analysis by considering how workers' decisions are influenced by wage rates.

Non-financial rewards
These 'rewards' can in fact be either positive or negative. Positive rewards include friendly colleagues, free sports facilities, and long holidays. Negative rewards include dirty or dangerous working conditions (negative rewards can also be termed 'costs').

> **Qu. 10.1** List the financial and non-financial rewards received by (*a*) an airline pilot, (*b*) a farm labourer, (*c*) a teacher.

Supply curve for labour

A supply curve shows the quantity of labour that would be supplied, in a given period, at various wage rates. (The non-financial rewards of the job are said to be given.) Figure 10.1 is a market supply curve, i.e. it relates to labour of a given type. It can be seen that no labour would be supplied at wage rates up to W. W represents the *transfer*

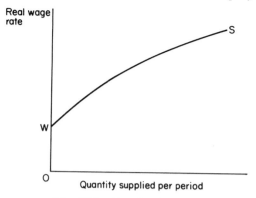

Fig. 10.1 Supply of labour

earnings of these workers (see below). Thereafter, the higher the wage rate, the more labour would be supplied.

Note that the amount of labour supplied depends upon the *real* wage rate. The real wage indicates the quantity of goods and services that can be purchased, which depends upon the money wage and the prices of goods and services.

It is easiest to illustrate this by means of index numbers. In the table below we start with an index of 100 for both money wage and prices. The money wage then rises by 20 per cent to 120. But since prices also rise by 20 per cent, the real wage is unchanged. If workers are aware that the real wage is unchanged, there is no reason to expect a change in the quantity of labour supplied.

Money wage index	Price index	Real wage index
100	100	100
120	120	120

Elasticity of supply

As we saw in Chapter 6, elasticity of supply is a measure of the responsiveness of supply to a change in price. The wage rate is the price of labour, and Figure 10.2 comprises several labour supply curves with differing elasticities.

Inelastic supply

S_2 denotes that the supply of labour is inelastic. This indicates that there are barriers which prevent large numbers of workers from moving into the market in response to higher wage rates (e.g.

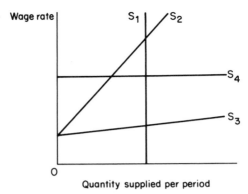

Fig. 10.2   Labour supply curves with differing elasticities

restrictions imposed by trade unions, or lengthy training periods, as for doctors).

Elastic supply
Supply is likely to be elastic (S_3) when the job entails skills that are widely distributed among the population (e.g. drivers) or are easily acquired (e.g. routine assembly operations). In such labour markets a slight increase in the wage rate leads to a more than proportionate increase in the quantity of labour supplied.

Perfectly inelastic and perfectly elastic supply
S_1 and S_4 represent the theoretical extremes of inelastic and elastic supply. S_1 indicates 'perfectly inelastic supply of labour', i.e. that a given amount of labour would be supplied whatever the wage rate. Conversely, S_4 represents a situation where increasing amounts of labour are supplied at a fixed wage rate; this would be 'perfectly elastic supply' of labour.

Significance of elasticity of supply

We saw in Chapter 6 that the demand for labour (as for other factors of production) depends upon the value of labour in use. A change in the value in use causes a change in demand. For example, an increase in demand for airline travel causes an increase in demand for airline pilots; a fall in demand for air travel causes a fall in demand for pilots.

The elasticity of supply determines the impact on wage rates of a given change in demand. Figure 10.3 contains two supply curves.

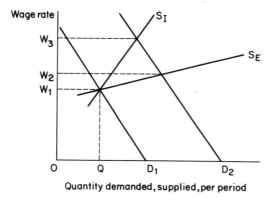

Fig. 10.3   Elasticity of supply and change in wage rate

The inelastic curve S_I refers to airline pilots, the elastic curve S_E refers to bus drivers. The difference in elasticity is due to two factors:

(*a*)   it takes far longer to train an airline pilot than a bus driver;
(*b*)   bus drivers can adapt more easily to other occupations (e.g. fork-lift truck drivers, packers, warehousemen) than can airline pilots.

Given the initial demand D_1, the wage rate is W_1 at which Q pilots and drivers are employed. When demand increases to D_2 the wage rate increases far less for drivers (W_2) than for pilots (W_3).

> **Qu. 10.2**   What factors influence the elasticity of supply of labour?

Position of the supply curve

Factors which influence the slope of the supply curve also affect its position. In Figure 10.4 (page 112) S_D is the supply curve for doctors, and S_L the supply curve for general labourers. Far more people have the abilities required to be a general labourer than a doctor. Moreover, not all of the people who *could* become doctors are willing to undertake the very long training involved. Finally, not all of the people who are willing and able to qualify as doctors can gain admittance to medical school, since the number of places is limited. Consequently the number of people in the 'doctors market' is much smaller than the number of people in the 'general labourers market'.

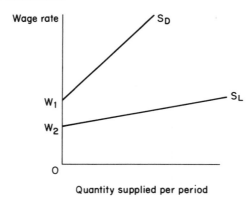

Fig. 10.4 Supply of doctors and labourers

Both doctors and labourers require a certain wage rate before they offer themselves for work. If we assume that labourers are the lowest paid workers in the country, their minimum acceptable wage rate W_2 will depend on the income that they would obtain if they did not work, e.g. from unemployment benefit. (If they enjoy their leisure the wage rate will have to be higher than the unemployment benefit to persuade them to work. However, if they dislike being idle they may wish to work even if their income would be higher if they were unemployed.)

The doctors' minimum wage rate W_1 is higher. This reflects the fact that they can earn W_1 in other occupations, e.g. in research, teaching, as medical representatives, etc. (Again an allowance has to be made for the relative attractions, the non-financial rewards, of the various occupations.)

A change in supply

Figure 10.5 refers to a given occupation. An increase in the labour supplied at any wage rate is indicated by a shift of the supply curve downward and to the right from S_1 to S_2. A fall in supply would be indicated by an upward shift in the curve, from S_2 to S_1.

An increase in supply

The shift of the supply curve from S_1 to S_2 could have been caused by various factors:

(*a*) A fall in unemployment benefit; some people who were previously satisfied to live on unemployment benefit now seek work.

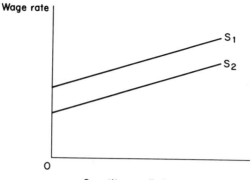

Fig. 10.5   Change in supply of labour

(b)   A fall in wage rates in other occupations.
(c)   A worsening of non-financial factors (e.g. working conditions) in other occupations.
(d)   An improvement in non-financial factors in this occupation.
(e)   An increase in the number of people willing and able to enter this occupation due, for example, to an increased population.
(f)   A lowering of entry standards or required qualifications, e.g. because of the de-skilling of jobs.

A fall in supply

A fall in the supply of labour to a given occupation could occur following changes opposite to those listed above, i.e. an increase in unemployment benefit, an increase in wage rates in other occupations, an improvement in non-financial factors in this occupation, a fall in the number of people willing and able to enter this occupation, and a raising of entry standards or required qualifications.

Qu. 10.3   What factors may cause the supply of a given type of labour to (a) increase, (b) decrease?

Importance of information

People will move from one occupation or job to another, in response to changes in relative rewards, only if they are aware of what these rewards are. This may seem obvious, but in practice people's information on this matter is far from perfect. There are three main reasons for a lack of information:

1   *The cost of acquiring information*   To acquire information
about wage rates, working conditions, promotion prospects, etc.,
may require substantial expenditure of time and money. Some
information can be obtained from government Jobcentres, private
employment agencies, and newspaper advertisements. But if it is
necessary to supplement this information by having interviews with
prospective employers, more time and expense are involved.
2   *Information requires personal experience*   There is some information about jobs that can be acquired only by working in those
jobs. For example, a person considering joining a firm may ask a
friend who works there about the other workers. However, one
person may get on very well with a given group of work-mates,
whereas another person might not fit at all with that group.
3   *Uncertainty due to time*   It is impossible to predict with
complete accuracy how relative rewards will change in the future.
At present the job prospects of people working with computers are
extremely favourable, since the demand for trained personnel is
rising faster than the supply. However, in twenty or thirty years'
time the situation could be quite different. If large numbers of
people enter the market, supply could outstrip demand.

The fact that people do not have perfect information has several
implications:

(*a*)   'Job search' is limited. Rather than spend a great deal of time
and money in trying to find the *best* job, people survey a
limited range of opportunities and settle for a job that is
satisfactory. The level of unemployment benefit and of redundancy pay can affect the degree of job search undertaken.
The higher these benefits are, the more time workers are likely
to take before applying for or accepting a new job.
(*b*)   Workers should expect to change their occupation as changes
occur in the demand for particular skills. At the moment we
are in a period of very rapid technological change, sometimes
known as the information revolution. Rapid technological
change requires even more frequent changes in the demand
for skills.
(*c*)   To prepare people for more frequent changes in occupation,
it may be necessary to increase the resources devoted to
re-training.

Qu. 10.4 Explain how a lack of information can affect the
labour market.

Economics of training

In principle we can see education as preparation for all aspects of life, including work and leisure, and training as preparation for work. However, there is clearly an overlap. Learning to read and write, learning how to get on with people, is useful both for work and for other aspects of our lives. Consequently, in practice we cannot always draw a clear dividing line between education and training. In this section we shall ignore this difficulty, and assume that we can identify a process called training whose objective is to prepare people for work.

Benefits of training

Training performs several functions:

(*a*) it prepares people to enter the labour force;
(*b*) it enables workers to perform their existing jobs more efficiently;
(*c*) it prepares workers for promotion;
(*d*) it enables people to change their occupation more easily (this is usually known as re-training, as noted above).

The benefits of this process are enjoyed by trainees, employers, and the community as a whole. For the people trained, the main benefit is a higher income, but more highly trained workers may also obtain greater job satisfaction. Employers benefit because a more highly trained workforce can produce a higher output, and better quality products.

In purely economic terms the benefit to the community can be measured by the change in output, already noted. But there may be additional benefits, e.g. a reduction in unemployment and the social unrest to which unemployment can give rise.

Costs of training

Two types of cost are involved. One is the financial cost of buildings, equipment, instructors, etc. The other cost is the output that the trainees *could* have produced during the period of training (the opportunity cost). The loss of output may be very small if training is given 'on the job'. It is much greater if the training is mainly in the classroom or laboratory. For example, people studying at university to become lawyers, engineers or doctors produce little or nothing for several years. This loss of output is usually reflected in the lower income received by trainees. Figure 10.6 illustrates this point. Line U refers to a person who undertakes little or no training. His – or her – income is zero (apart from casual earnings and pocket money,

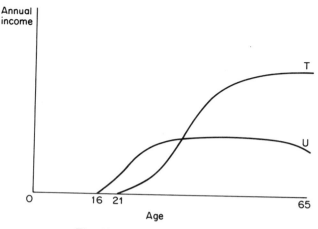

Fig. 10.6   Training and income

ignored here) up to the age of 16. He then leaves school and takes a job. His earnings rise quite rapidly at first with increasing age and experience, but then level off and for most of his working life are roughly constant. Earnings may fall a little as he approaches retirement.

Line T refers to a person who undergoes extensive training. He stays on at school for another two or three years and then goes to college. During this time his income from employment is assumed to be zero (an assumption that we relax below). However, once he is trained, his income soon rises above that of the untrained person and continues to be higher for the rest of his working life.

The total expected lifetime earnings are considerably higher for the trained than for the untrained person and we might therefore expect that all people who are able to undertake training successfully would do so. However, it must be remembered that the earnings curves are only projections. As noted earlier, substantial changes in a given labour market can arise within one person's lifetime. Consequently people may heavily discount the higher earnings that may occur in future years. They may pay more attention to, say, the first eight or ten years, when the untrained person has the higher overall earnings.

The result of this would, of course, be a reduction in the number of people coming forward for training. If the benefits of training were enjoyed only by those trained, it is possible that no action would be taken to change the situation. However, as we have seen, training also benefits employers and the community as a whole.

Consequently employers and governments often reduce the cost of training to the individual, and thus increase the balance of benefits over costs.

Government assistance for training

The form of government assistance varies from one country to another but usually comprises two elements:

(*a*) provision of free or subsidised facilities (equipment, staff, etc.), and
(*b*) grants and loans to students and other trainees.

So, for example, in the UK students on degree courses receive a grant, the value of which depends upon their parents' income, and do not pay fees. (This means that their income is positive and not zero as assumed in Figure 10.6.) Unemployed people may be able to attend free training courses administered by the government and receive an income while doing so.

Employers' assistance

Employers may provide training facilities, and they may finance employees to attend courses either in or outside their working time. The training provided by an employer may take two forms:

(*a*) Training specific to the worker's current employment. New employees often attend courses to familiarise themselves with the firm's procedures; salesmen are trained to understand the products that they are selling. This training is of benefit to both employer and employee.
(*b*) More general training relating to the trainee's occupation. Professional firms, such as accountants, frequently finance junior employees' professional studies. In this instance it is more difficult to ensure that the firm benefits from the training. Once the student becomes professionally qualified he or she may find other employment.

If all employers provide roughly the same level of assistance (in proportion to their size), then for each firm losses and gains arising from moves by employees may balance. But this does not always happen. One of the features of the UK Industrial Training Act was the imposition of a levy on firms which did not do sufficient training, especially of apprentices, to meet their needs and who relied on attracting trained workers from other employers.

> **Qu. 10.5** Discuss the proposition that since workers benefit from training they should bear the cost.

Qu. 10.6   What factors might influence the choice of a school leaver between continuing in education and beginning work?

Qu. 10.7   Discuss the case for replacing student grants by loans to be repaid after the student has found employment.

Employee and employer organisations

We have concentrated in this chapter on the activities of individual workers and employers. But we should recognise the importance of collective organisations which represent groups of workers or employers.

Trade unions

The main economic purpose of unions is to negotiate the terms and conditions of service of their members. As we saw above, if the wage rate is negotiated centrally by the union and all workers adhere to the agreement, the supply of labour is perfectly elastic at that wage rate (line S_4 in Figure 10.2).

We have also seen that unions and professional bodies, such as the British Medical Association, may influence the supply of labour by imposing restrictions on entry to the labour market. For example, a union may try to ensure that particular jobs are done only by workers accredited as skilled by the union. Moreover, the union may try to stipulate the length of the training period required.

There are, of course, advantages in having a highly trained labour force. But unions have sometimes tried to maintain longer training periods than were needed, in order to restrict the number of skilled workers. In recent years, following pressure from employers, there has been a considerable reduction in the length of engineering apprenticeships in the UK. Moreover, many of the traditional boundaries between training in mechanical and electrical engineering have been broken. Workers who have acquired more than one skill are better able to adjust to rapid technological change.

Unions often cooperate with employers in connection with the introduction of new technology or different working practices. But *on the whole* British unions have been less willing to cooperate than unions in other countries such as the USA and West Germany. This is believed to be one of the reasons why productivity levels are lower in the UK than in these other countries.

Qu. 10.8   Explain how trade unions can affect the labour market.

Employers' organisations

Firms in some British industries have formed employers' associations (e.g. the Engineering Employers' Federation) to negotiate with trade unions on wages, conditions of employment, etc. They also make representations to the government concerning the level of imports, government assistance etc.

Alternative definitions of work

We have focused so far on work that is undertaken in return for a wage or salary. But such work accounts for a smaller proportion of people's lives (and especially men's lives) than previously. Many people spend time on other activities which make a contribution to the economic welfare of the community. (Although these activities do not constitute work as defined above, they are often considered as work by the people concerned.) These other economically useful activities include:

1 *Activities within the home* The most important of these are the many activities undertaken by housewives (often with the help of other members of the family). It also includes do-it-yourself activities such as painting and decorating. DIY has become more important in recent years, partly because of improvements in equipment and partly because of a shortening of the (paid) working week.

The main beneficiary of these activities is the household undertaking them. But there may also be external benefits (e.g. a well-maintained house with an attractive garden gives more pleasure to passers-by than a house with peeling paint-work and a garden full of weeds).

2 *Charitable activities* There is an enormous range of activities that might be classified as charitable in the sense that they are not of benefit primarily to the people undertaking them. They include working in charity shops, the meals-on-wheels service for infirm people, clearing litter from areas of natural beauty, and teaching English to immigrants.

Many of these activities have traditionally been undertaken by housewives whose husbands met the family's financial needs. But unemployed people (men and women) have become increasingly involved in charitable activities, either informally on their own initiative or formally through job-creation schemes.

These developments mean that the distinction between 'work' and 'leisure' activities is becoming blurred. No longer can work be equated with paid activities, and leisure with unpaid activities. If unemployment remains high in the future, a further blurring of the distinction can be expected.

11

Finance

We examined decisions on expenditure in Chapter 1 and the nature and role of money in Chapter 3. We now extend the discussion by examining the sources of finance available to households, producers and governments. We discuss each of these groups separately, but we first establish the framework for this discussion.

Income, expenditure and saving

We start with the basic relationship:

Income = expenditure + saving

Note that saving may be positive (income exceeds expenditure) or negative (expenditure exceeds income). Moreover, for any member of the three groups, and for the group as a whole, saving may be positive at certain times and negative at others, as changes occur in the stream of income and/or expenditure.

As we saw in Chapter 1, a household's needs, and hence its expenditure, fluctuate as changes occur in the size of the household and the ages of the various members. In a similar way, a firm's expenditure will vary as it changes its output, introduces new products and so forth.

In the following sections we examine the sources from which each group can obtain finance, and the forms of saving undertaken by each group. We also show how decisions taken by the three groups interact. Figure 11.1 shows that the pattern of interaction is complex. There are direct two-way financial flows between households and producers, producers and the government and the government and households. In addition, there is a series of indirect flows via financial intermediaries such as banks and insurance companies.

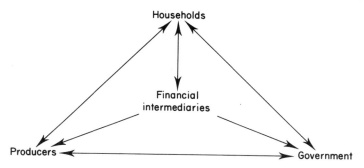

Fig. 11.1 Financial flows

Sources of finance for households

If households wish to spend more than their current income, they can borrow money from several sources. Borrowing can be broadly classified as long, medium or short term.

Long-term borrowing

For most households the largest item of expenditure financed by borrowing is the purchase of a house or flat. This is usually financed by a mortgage from a building society or bank. The title-deeds to the property are made over to the building society or bank for the duration of the loan, which is usually for a period of up to 25 years.

In the UK the interest payments on mortgages up to a certain level are offset against the borrower's liability to income tax. Thus the government in effect subsidises this form of borrowing. The subsidy is usually justified on the ground that home ownership is socially desirable.

Medium-term borrowing

Expenditure on consumer durables – cars, washing machines, etc. – can be financed from a number of sources. Banks provide overdrafts or personal loans (the banks prefer the latter because they attract a higher rate of interest). Alternatively, goods may be obtained on hire purchase, the money being provided by finance companies. Or goods may be purchased on credit, provided by the manufacturer (common for cars) or the retailer (common for household goods). Manufacturers and retailers may in turn obtain finance from finance companies for which, in effect, they act as agents. Money borrowed for the purchase of consumer durables is usually repaid over two or three years, although overdrafts are usually arranged for shorter periods.

Short-term borrowing
Even shorter term finance is available through credit cards issued either by banks or retailers. Credit is free if payment is made within a few weeks after purchase. Thereafter interest is payable at a high rate.

Saving by households

The financial intermediaries which lend money to households also accept their savings. Banks and building societies now compete more vigorously for deposits than previously. They offer a wider range of savings opportunities, paying higher rates of interest on bigger sums and on sums deposited for longer periods.

Some households channel part of their savings to producers by buying debentures (a form of lending) or shares (thus becoming part-owners of the company). They may also lend money to the government, e.g. by buying national savings certificates or bonds.

Finally, many households contribute to life assurance and pension schemes. These contributions combine saving with insurance against risk. The insurance companies and pension funds invest these contributions in various ways, including the purchase of shares, debentures and government bonds.

> **Qu. 11.1**   From which sources are households most likely to borrow in order to finance the purchase of (*a*) houses, (*b*) cars, (*c*) clothes, (*d*) food?
>
> **Qu. 11.2**   Do you think it desirable that interest payments can be offset against income tax when money is borrowed to finance the purchase of a house, but not when it is borrowed to finance the purchase of children's clothes?
>
> **Qu. 11.3**   Describe the main forms of saving by households.

Sources of finance for producers

We use the term 'producers', rather than 'firms', to distinguish them from financial intermediaries. (The financing of these intermediaries is considered below.) The sources of finance that are available depend upon the producer's legal status (see Chapter 8).

Sole traders and partnerships use the same sources of finance as households: mortgages, bank loans and overdrafts, hire-purchase finance and trade credit. These are all forms of borrowing.

Companies also borrow in these ways, although long-term borrowing is usually via the issue of debentures, rather than via mortgages. In addition, companies usually obtain permanent capital through the issue of shares. We saw above that some household saving is channelled, directly or via financial intermediaries, into the purchase of shares and debentures.

The shareholders are the owners of the company concerned. The right to transfer shares is restricted by the articles of association of some private companies. But in most instances there are no restrictions, and shares can be bought and sold freely. However, shareholders do not have the right to sell their shares back to the company; as we said earlier, share capital is permanent capital.

The capital market

In most industrialised countries a complex capital market has developed to ease the flow of finance from savers to companies. Central to this market is the stock exchange. As an example of the operation of a stock exchange let us consider the London Stock Exchange.

The London Stock Exchange

The Stock Exchange is the market where company securities – shares and debentures – are traded. (Government securities are also traded on the London Exchange.) Every day, Monday to Friday, some 20 000 to 25 000 deals are transacted, with a total value of around £500 millions. The trading is undertaken by firms which are members of the Stock Exchange (although some members are owned by non-member firms). These firms can deal direct with investors (savers), buying and selling securities from their own 'book', or they can act as agents, buying and selling on behalf of clients.

All the trading is of *existing* securities and does not in itself raise any new money for companies. However, the existence of a market for securities means that it is very much easier for companies to obtain money in the first place by issuing securities. People would be far more reluctant to buy securities if there was not a market in which these securities could be sold when required.

> **Qu. 11.4** Explain how the stock exchange contributes to economic welfare.

The new issue market

In order to raise additional finance, new securities (shares or debentures) must be issued. New issues may take several forms:

1 *Public issue by prospectus* The company offers, direct to the

general public, a fixed number of securities at a stated price. A prospectus is issued, setting out the nature of the company's business and giving details of past turnover and profits.

2   *Offer for sale*   This is similar to the public issue, but the company sells the securities to an issuing house (usually a merchant bank), which in turn offers them to the general public.

3   *Placing*   The securities are again acquired by an issuing house, which offers them to its clients, usually large institutions such as insurance companies. To reduce the possibility that these institutions may make substantial profits when the securities are subsequently traded on the Stock Exchange, the authorities stipulate that a minimum quantity be initially placed with the market-makers for sale to the general public.

4   *Offer for sale by tender*   This method tends to be used when it is particularly difficult to judge how investors will respond to a new issue, e.g. if it is the first time that the company has issued securities to the public. A minimum price is stated at which a tender will be accepted. If investors believe that the securities are worth more than the minimum price, they will put in a higher offer in order to try to secure an allocation.

5   *Rights issue*   A rights issue is confined to the company's existing shareholders, who are offered additional shares in proportion to their holdings. The new shares are issued at a price below the current market price, and this can be seen as a reward to shareholders. A compensating benefit to the company is that the administrative costs are lower than for alternative methods.

Rights issues should not be confused with bonus or scrip issues. These also involve the issue of additional shares to existing shareholders, but since they are issued free, no new finance is raised.

Qu. 11.5   Explain the following: (*a*) offer for sale by tender, (*b*) rights issue, (*c*) bonus issue.

Underwriting

Companies issue securities at prices at which they expect these securities to be bought. But they may misjudge investors' attitudes and set too high a price. To ensure that it gets the money it needs, the company arranges that one or more underwriters – substantial financial institutions – will take up any securities not bought by the general public. In order to compensate for the fact that they may be required to take up stock that has subsequently to be sold at a loss, the underwriters charge a small commission related to the total value of the issue.

Unlisted securities market

In the mid-1970s the flow of new companies seeking a quotation on the London Stock Exchange all but ceased, partly because of the costs incurred and the conditions imposed. To overcome these obstacles the Stock Exchange introduced the Unlisted Securities Market in 1980. The USM requires a minimum of only 10 per cent of shares to be made available to the general public (as compared to 25 per cent for the main market), and a company can come to the market with only three instead of five years' trading (or even less for well researched high-technology companies). Companies have entered the USM at a rate of over eighty a year. These companies are on average much smaller than those on the main Stock Exchange, and the USM thus fulfils a useful function in channelling finance to smaller companies.

Financial intermediaries

The financial intermediaries identified in Figure 11.1 help to channel savers' funds to companies in various ways. Banks accept deposits and lend money to companies. Merchant banks act as issuing houses and offer general advice on new issues; finance houses specialise in hire-purchase finance; insurance companies act as underwriters. Another very important function is discussed in the following section.

Shareholders

A feature of modern capitalism is that an increasing proportion of company securities is held by institutional investors. Those investors are especially important in the UK where they hold about 60 per cent of shares, as compared to around 35 per cent in the USA. The major institutional shareholders are listed below.

Pension funds
An increasing number of firms pay pensions to their former employees. Contributions are made by both employer and employee, and the pension paid is usually a certain proportion of the employee's final salary. These contributions are invested in a variety of assets, including shares, and pension funds now account for almost 30 per cent of total shareholdings in the UK.

Insurance companies
As noted earlier in the chapter, many contributions to insurance companies are partly an insurance against risk and partly a form of

saving. In recent years contributions have increased and insurance companies have devoted a greater proportion of their funds to the purchase of shares. They now hold around one-fifth of total shares in the UK.

Unit trusts and investment trusts
Since share prices constantly fluctuate, the holding of shares is inherently risky. To reduce the degree of risk, shares may be purchased in a large number of companies. People may also purchase the units issued by unit trusts or the shares of investment trusts. This is an alternative way of spreading risk, since unit trusts and investment trusts themselves hold shares in a large number of companies.

> **Qu. 11.6** Discuss the role in a modern economy of financial intermediaries.

Saving by companies

Saving by companies takes two main forms:

1 *Depreciation allowances* As assets such as machines and equipment are used, they gradually wear out. Depreciation allowances are intended to build up a fund out of which replacement assets can be purchased.
2 *Undistributed profits* Companies seldom distribute all their profits as dividends to shareholders. They often 'plough back' a substantial proportion into the business. For many companies their own saving exceeds total external finance. Nevertheless external finance can be very important, especially for companies wishing to expand.

Sources of government finance

Governments obtain most of their revenue through taxation, a topic that is dealt with in detail in Chapter 16. But they frequently have to borrow to meet a gap between expenditure and tax revenue. Forms of borrowing include:

1 *Bonds (gilt edged stock)* These are issued by central government and the local authorities. These are long-term loans, usually carrying a fixed rate of interest. They may be issued initially either to financial institutions or to the general public, and are subsequently traded on the Stock Exchange.
2 *Treasury Bills* This is a much shorter form of borrowing, typically being for months rather than years. In the UK Bills are

offered weekly by tender and the imposition of a minimum size of tender effectively confines the market to large financial institutions.
3   There are various other forms of borrowing, the relative import-ance of which varies from one country to another. These include National Savings Certificates, deposits made with local authorities, and deposits made with publicly owned banks.

Government saving

On the rare occasions when revenue from taxation exceeds govern-ment expenditure, governments are able to repay some of the debts incurred in earlier years.

National debt

The national debt is the total debt incurred to date by the central government. It is *not* the amount owed by one country to another. Some government securities may be purchased by overseas investors, but most are held by the country's own citizens.

In many countries the national debt has risen over time, and this has given rise to considerable debate. It is sometimes claimed that governments should not borrow to finance projects that benefit today's citizens, when part of the cost of that borrowing – interest and redemption of the debt – falls on a future generation of citizens. On the other hand, future citizens also share in the benefits of this spending. They will travel on roads built today, enjoy freedom from occupation by foreign troops because of today's spending on defence, and so forth.

> **Qu. 11.7**   'Neither a borrower nor a lender be.' Do you think that this maxim should apply to (*a*) households, (*b*) producers, (*c*) governments?
>
> **Qu. 11.8**   Define the national debt and explain its existence.

Banking systems

We have left a discussion of banking systems until the end of the chapter since banks play an important role with regard to all three of the groups considered above: households, companies (producers) and governments. In all mixed economies the banking system comprises a number of commercial banks and a central bank.

Commercial banks

The role of commercial banks has been described, rather im-politely, as to 'borrow cheap and lend dear'. In fact, all banks need to attract money more cheaply than they lend or invest it, in order to cover their costs of administration. For most banks the major cost is maintaining the network of branches through which they maintain contact with the public.

Bank liabilities

Banks, like other companies, obtain money from their share-holders. But most of their funds comprise deposits. Bank deposits act as:

1   A convenient and safe form of holding money, especially when held as a current account (sight or demand deposits).
2   A form of saving, when held as a deposit account (time or saving deposits).

Bank assets

In choosing their mix of assets, banks have to bear in mind the need for:

1   *Liquidity*   In order to m   i the day-to-day demands of their depositors, banks maintain a small proportion of their assets in the form of notes and coin. In banks with a branch network, cash is held in each of the branches. As a first line of defence, to meet un-expected needs, banks hold assets which can be converted into cash very quickly (e.g. Treasury Bills which are very close to the date of maturity).
2   *Profitability*   In general the most profitable form of assets are advances (personal loans and overdrafts) and investments (bonds and shares – although UK banks have traditionally bought few shares). Prudent banks ensure that they do not pursue profitability to the point where their liquidity is threatened. This means that they limit the proportion of their assets accounted for by less liquid assets and carefully monitor their clients' liquidity. (In recent years some US banks suffered when farmers were unable to repay loans because of a fall in the price of agricultural produce.)
3   *Adherence to government policy*   Governments frequently control banks' activities. The various methods of control are discussed in Chapter 16.

Central banks

All modern banking systems have a central bank, e.g. the Bank of England (UK), Federal Reserve Bank (USA), Bundesbank (West Germany). The responsibilities of most central banks include:

(*a*) Control of the money supply and interest rates (a responsibility exercised in conjunction with the relevant government department),
(*b*) Acting as banker to the government,
(*c*) Acting as banker to the commercial banks,
(*d*) Supervision of commercial banks.

Qu. 11.9 What factors influence the assets held by commercial banks?

12

Income and Wealth Creation

We began this book by examining the decisions and activities of individuals and small groups. We then discussed the means by which these activities are brought together; this discussion involved a study of the markets for goods, labour and finance. In this chapter we take the analysis a stage further by examining how the activities of households, producers and the government interact to create income and wealth.

The distinction between income and wealth

It is said, with some truth, that 'the best things in life are free'. However, economics takes a rather narrow view of income and wealth by excluding many things which are free (e.g. love and friendship). We can consider income and wealth from various viewpoints, and in each instance we see that wealth is a *stock* and income is a *flow* arising from that stock.

Households
The major item of wealth of most households is the abilities and skills of those members of the household of working age. These abilities and skills are known as human capital. The stock of human capital varies from one household to another, and these differences give rise to differences in wages and salaries, i.e. in the flow of income.

Households have other assets, such as houses, cars and television sets, which yield a flow of benefits. These benefits may take the form of a monetary flow, as when a house or part of a house is rented out. But usually the benefits are taken 'in kind'. Houses provide their owners with shelter, cars provide transportation, television sets provide entertainment.

Finally, some households hold stocks of financial assets (e.g. shares and debentures) which yield income in the form of dividends and interest. However, although financial assets are an important part of the wealth of some households, they are not counted as part of wealth or capital as defined in economics. The reason for this is explained in the following section.

Producers

Assets owned by producers include factories, offices, machines and vehicles. To utilise these assets, producers hire workers (human capital). The assets are used to produce goods and services which yield a flow of revenue or income when sold.

In order to develop their businesses, producers obtain finance from households in exchange for financial securities (e.g. shares). If we included these securities *and* the assets bought with the money raised by issuing these securities, we would be guilty of 'double-counting', i.e. we would overestimate the nation's wealth. Consequently, as noted in the previous section, paper securities are excluded from economic wealth.

Government

Many important assets are owned by central or local government, acting on behalf of the nation's citizens. These assets, such as roads, schools, and hospitals, constitute the *infrastructure* of the economy. They provide flows of benefits or services. In principle, these services could be sold to provide revenue for the government. In practice, as we have seen in earlier chapters, many are provided at a low, and often a zero, price.

National wealth and income

A nation's stock of wealth comprises the wealth or assets of all households, all producers and the government. The national income comprises the income derived from these assets.

Qu. 12.1 Distinguish between income and wealth, and say which is a stock and which a flow.

Qu. 12.2 List wealth of (*a*) your household, (*b*) your school, college, firm or any other organisation with which you are familiar.

In the following sections we explain how the stock of *assets* and the flow of *income* may *change* over time. But in order to do this it is helpful first to examine an economy with a constant, *unchanging* flow of *income*.

A simple model of an economy

Figure 12.1 presents a two-sector model of an economy (the government sector being ignored for the moment). The diagram shows that households supply labour to producers (flow A), in exchange for wages and salaries (flow B). The producers use this labour, together with their other assets (e.g. machines), to produce goods and services. These goods and services are sold to households (flow C) in exchange for money (flow D).

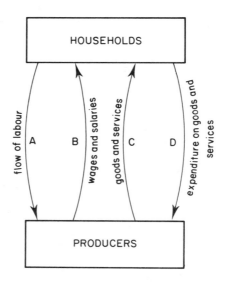

Fig. 12.1   Simple model of an economy

National income

In principle, the four flows shown in Figure 12.1 constitute alternative measures of the national income. In practice, in most countries national income is measured in three ways, via the income approach (corresponding to flow B), the output approach (flow C), and the expenditure approach (flow D).

One important thing to note about this diagram is that *all four* flows are of equal magnitude. For example, if in a given year the income of households was £100 billions, we know that their expenditure would also be £100 billions.

Equilibrium national income

Two things are indicated by the term 'equilibrium':

(*a*) The fulfilment of plans, e.g. producers sell the amount they plan to sell; consumers spend the amount they plan to spend.

(*b*) A situation of stability. When national income reaches an equilibrium level, there is no tendency for it to change; this point is reached when *planned expenditure in one period equals income in the previous period.*

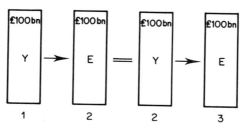

Fig. 12.2 Equilibrium national income

A situation of stability is depicted in Figure 12.2. We start in period 1 with an income of £100 billions. In period 2 planned and actual expenditure is £100 billions (i.e. expenditure plans are fulfilled). For the reason explained above, income must therefore also be £100 billions. This income gives rise to planned and actual expenditure in period 3 of £100 billions (producers' plans are also fulfilled since they expected to sell the same amount as in the previous period). Moreover, the other condition for equilibrium, that planned expenditure in one period should equal income in the previous period, is also fulfilled.

> **Qu. 12.3** Define equilibrium national income. What conditions must be fulfilled if national income is to reach an equilibrium level?

Disequilibrium

Disequilibrium exists when some plans are *not fulfilled*, and planned expenditure in one period does *not* equal income in the previous period. Consider the situation where households, having satisfied some of their needs, plan to spend 90 per cent instead of 100 per cent of their income. If producers plan their output on the assumption that consumers will continue to spend all of their income, these

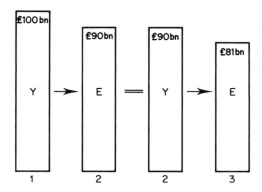

Fig. 12.3   Declining national income

plans will be frustrated. (This will be manifested in an unplanned increase in stocks.)

This situation is illustrated in Figure 12.3. From an income of £100 billions in period 1, £90 billions is spent in period 2, £10 billions less than expected by producers.

Two things should be noted about this situation. First, equilibrium may not be re-established for a long time. For example, producers, observing that expenditure in period 2 is £90 billions, may expect that to continue in period 3. However, it can be seen that expenditure falls again in period 3, to £81 billions. The outcome of these unfulfilled expectations will be a further increase in unsold stocks of goods.

The other thing to note is that the economy shown here is gradually 'winding down', as expenditure, income and output (and also employment) continue to decline. This decline will continue as long as expenditure is less than the previous period's income. On the other hand, equilibrium will be restored once all income is spent (provided, of course, that producers plan to sell the required amount).

Re-establishment of equilibrium

In the simple model that we have been considering so far, all expenditure is undertaken by households. In this situation equilibrium will be re-established when households' income falls to the level at which they have to spend all of it to meet their needs.

When we consider a more complex and realistic model of a national economy we see that expenditure is undertaken not only by households but also by producers and the government. Examples of spending by producers and the government have been given in earlier chapters. (In Chapter 15 we examine a more complex model that takes account of exports and imports.)

Saving (i.e. income exceeds expenditure) by households may be balanced by dissaving (i.e. expenditure exceeds income) by producers or the government, as illustrated in Figure 12.4. National income in period 1 is £100 billions. Of this income £50 billions is received by households, and £25 billions each by producers and the government.

In this example, households spend 90 per cent of their income, i.e. £45 billions. This *consumption* expenditure is designated C. Producers spend £28 billions, £3 billions more than their income. This *investment* expenditure is designated I. Finally the government spends £27 billions, £2 billions more than its income. This *government expenditure on goods and services* is designated G.

Aggregating the three expenditure flows we have:

$$E = C + I + G$$
$$= \text{£bn } 45 + 28 + 27$$
$$= \text{£bn } 100$$

Expenditure in period 2 equals income in period 1, indicating a situation of equilibrium. This occurs because producers and the government borrow money saved by households and spend this money on goods and services.

In this example we can identify another way of expressing the condition for equilibrium, namely that in a given period *planned expenditure* financed by borrowing equals *planned saving*:

$$\text{£bn } 3 + 2 = 5$$

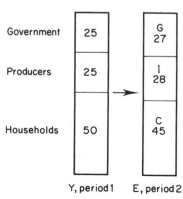

Fig. 12.4 Income and aggregate expenditure

> **Qu. 12.4**   What is incorrect in the following definition? Expenditure equals consumption plus investment minus government spending on goods and services.

Equilibrium and employment

The fact that the economy is in equilibrium does *not* mean that the situation is necessarily satisfactory. Equilibrium may be reached even though productive resources are unused, e.g. workers remain unemployed. Some economists claim that this would be only a temporary equilibrium, and that market forces would eventually lead to full employment.

Other economists are less optimistic and believe that governments may need to intervene to modify market forces in order to increase the level of economic activity and in particular the level of employment. Since we discuss government policy in later chapters it is sufficient to note here that the forms of intervention usually advocated are:

(*a*)   An increase in government expenditure
(*b*)   Measures, such as lower taxation and interest rates, designed to encourage expenditure by households and producers.

> **Qu. 12.5**   Explain the relationship, if any, between the equilibrium level of national income and full employment.

Limits to expenditure and output

In the previous section we considered situations where expenditure was considered to be too low because it left labour and other resources unemployed. In other instances expenditure may be considered to be too high because it gives rise to inflationary tendencies, i.e. to increasing costs and prices. Inflation tends to occur when output approaches the limit set by the nation's economic capacity. These two situations of too low and too high a level of expenditure, can be illustrated by means of the production possibility boundary.

Production possibility boundary

Figure 12.5 shows the various combinations of products that an economy could produce in a given period, e.g. a year. The many thousand types of goods and services can be classified under one of two headings:

(*a*)   *Consumption goods*, e.g. food, consumer durables, entertainment.

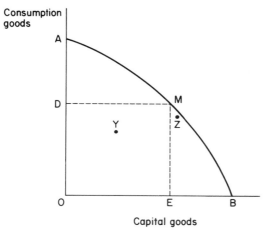

Fig. 12.5 Production possibility boundary

(*b*) *Capital goods*, e.g. machines, components, raw materials.

If in the economy modelled in Figure 12.5 all resources were employed and working at maximum efficiency, it would be possible to produce OA consumption goods or OB capital goods or any combination represented by a point on the production possibility boundary (or curve) AB. For example, point M would represent an output of OD consumption goods plus OE capital goods.

The combination Y would illustrate the first situation discussed above, where expenditure is low and there are substantial unused resources. On the other hand if expenditure was high and output Z was produced inflation might well result because the margin of used resources is very small indeed. (We have shown in earlier chapters that a high level of demand is frequently associated with increases in the price of products and of labour.)

Faced with this latter situation the government may well try to reduce the level of expenditure in order to counteract inflation, even though this would mean increasing the level of unemployed resources including labour. (Again the methods that might be used are discussed in later chapters.)

It would also be possible to increase the level of unused resources, and hence counteract inflation, by expanding the nation's economic capacity. This is illustrated by the outward shift of the production possibility boundary to $A^1 B^1$ in Figure 12.6 (page 138). Indeed, an expansion of economic capacity might enable output to be increased

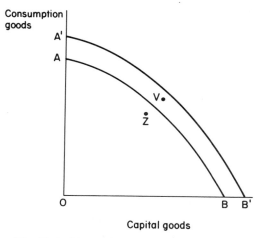

Fig. 12.6　Expansion of economic capacity

(e.g. from Z to V) without adding to inflation. The mechanisms by which economic capacity might be expanded are discussed in the following chapter.

Qu. 12.6　Describe the circumstances in which the government might try to reduce aggregate expenditure, and explain what undesirable effects might follow.

13

Economic Growth and Development

Introduction

In the previous chapter we examined the process of wealth and income creation. We showed that one measure of a country's income is the output of goods and services. The higher the output, the higher the national income. Output can be increased up to the limit set by the nation's economic capacity. Thereafter output can increase only if economic capacity expands.

In this chapter we extend the analysis by examining the relationship between an increase in national income, economic growth and economic development. We begin by considering the meaning of economic growth.

Economic growth

Economic growth is defined differently by different economists. Some define it as an *increase in output* or in *national income*, others as an *expansion of economic capacity*. The difference between these two definitions can be illustrated by reference to Figure 13.1 (p. 140).

In period 1, with economic capacity represented by the production possibility boundary A B, output increases from J to K. This constitutes economic growth on the first but not the second definition.

In period 2 economic capacity expands, as shown by the shift of the production possibility boundary from AB to A^1B^1. This constitutes economic growth on the second definition, even if output remains at K. Only when output increases from K to L does economic growth occur on the first definition.

Economic development

The term economic growth can be applied to all countries, rich and poor, whereas economic development is usually applied to the

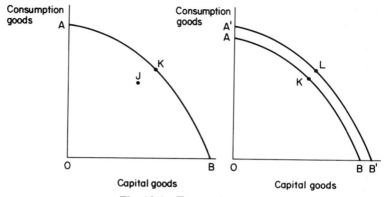

Fig. 13.1   Economic growth

poorer, or less developed countries. Economic growth, as we shall see later, is required for, but does not guarantee, economic development.

Expansion of economic capacity

Although there are different definitions of economic growth, it is clear that a *sustained* increase in output, and hence in national income, requires an expansion of economic capacity. An expansion of economic capacity can result either from an increase in the *productivity* of existing resources or from an increase in the *quantity* of resources. In practice these two developments often occur together. For the sake of clarity, however, we shall analyse them separately here.

> **Qu. 13.1**   Explain why an expansion of economic capacity is required for a sustained increase in national income.

Increase in productivity

Productivity is the ratio of output to input. Many factors can give rise to an increase in productivity, to an increase in the quantity of output obtained from a given amount of resources. One of the most important factors is an improvement in the *quality of capital inputs*. This can occur as newer vintages of a given type of equipment replace older vintages, as noted in Chapter 2. Quality also improves when a given type of equipment is replaced by a different type. For example, automatic transfer devices and robots are becoming widespread in car assembly plants and in engineering, while in offices we have seen the manual typewriter give way to the electric typewriter, the electronic typewriter, and the word processor.

The *quality of human capital* can also be improved through education and training of the workforce, or simply through experience. For example experience can point the way to better production planning and an improved factory layout, leading to a smoother flow of work.

Qu. 13.2   How may changes in the quality of inputs occur?

Increase in the quantity of resources

We discussed in Chapter 2 the factors influencing the quantity of resources and hence the flow of inputs. Significant changes in the *supply of labour* can occur over long time periods. But in the short term, changes in the *amount of capital* installed are likely to be more important. Moreover if economic capacity expands because of an increase in the supply of labour following an increase in population, *total national income* may increase without a corresponding increase *in national income per head*. This could increase, fall or remain constant, depending on the overall composition of the population. (See the discussion of optimum population in Chapter 2.)

A country's stock of capital – machines, buildings, roads etc. – constantly *depreciates* (becomes depleted) through use. Consequently some investment is required each year to make good this depreciation, to maintain the existing economic capacity. When investment exceeds depreciation, the stock of capital assets, and hence economic capacity, increases.

In the mid-1980s investment expenditure in the UK was about £60 billions a year. Depreciation was almost £40 billions, leaving net investment around £20 billions. This £20 billions of expenditure represented the increase in the stock of capital assets, the expansion of economic capacity.

Qu. 13.3   Explain how an expansion of economic capacity can occur.

Qu. 13.4   Discuss the relationship between investment, depreciation and economic capacity.

Current versus future consumption

If there is spare economic capacity (*unemployed resources*), it may be possible to increase the output of capital goods without reducing the output of consumption goods. But if there is insufficient spare capacity, it will be necessary to curtail consumption in order to release resources for the capital goods industries. This situation is

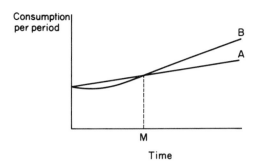

Fig. 13.2   Alternative consumption paths

illustrated in Figure 13.2, which shows two alternative time paths for consumption.

Path A shows a steady increase in consumption through time. Path B shows that at the beginning of the period consumption declines in order to 'make room' for a higher rate of investment and a faster rate of growth of economic capacity. Subsequently, as the additional capacity comes 'on stream', it is possible to increase consumption at a faster rate than on time path A. The two paths cross at time period M, and beyond M consumption is higher on path B.

In choosing between future and current consumption several factors have to be taken into account:

1   Does the sacrifice of current consumption require an absolute fall in consumption, as shown in Figure 13.2, or merely a reduction in its rate of growth? It will probably be easier to make the sacrifice in the second than the first situation.

2   What is the initial level of consumption? It is especially difficult to reduce consumption when some people are already on the 'bread line', as in some less developed countries. Ironically these are the countries which are in greatest need of additional investment. As we show in Chapter 14, many of these countries feel unable to make reductions in consumption and rely on economic aid to finance investment.

3   What is the time scale? Referring again to Figure 13.2, it will be easier to make the sacrifice in consumption if point M is reached in two rather than in twenty years; a twenty year period would imply that a considerable proportion of the existing population would not live to enjoy the benefits of their sacrifice.

4   Finally it should be recognised that government intervention (e.g. the imposition of taxes or the introduction of rationing) is

likely to be required in order to reduce consumption. The policy might therefore be opposed on political grounds.

Qu. 13.5   What factors might influence the choice between current and future consumption?

Forms of economic growth

Our simplified model, Figure 13.1, distinguished between the two broad categories of capital and consumption goods, and showed that economic growth enables a choice to be made between an increase in the output of one or other category, or of both. Economic growth also widens the range of choices within each category, as shown in the following sections.

Composition of consumption

Economic growth frequently involves the introduction of new products and improved versions of existing products. One of the most important new products ever to be introduced was the motor car, about a century ago. Since then there have been innumerable refinements to the basic model: full protection from weather for the passengers, heating, windscreen wipers, improved brakes, higher performance engines, etc.

The introduction of a new (or improved) product can have differing effects on existing products. At one extreme a new product can be supplied and purchased without any appreciable change in the output and sales of existing products. All or virtually all of the additional capacity devoted to the new product constitutes economic growth.

In most instances, however, increased spending on new (or improved) products involves less spending on existing products. This implies a corresponding transfer of resources from the production of existing to new products. In these instances the net growth in economic capacity is the capacity devoted to the new products *minus* the reduction in the capacity devoted to existing products. For example, the fashion for 'healthy eating' led to a higher output of wholemeal bread and a lower output of white bread.

Sometimes new products have such clear advantages over existing products that the production of these existing products falls dramatically and perhaps ceases entirely. The increase in car ownership led to a decline in the sales of horse-drawn carriages. Since the advent of the pocket calculator very few slide rules have been produced.

In many instances, however, the impact is less dramatic; new and existing products fight a prolonged battle. Plastics and metals have competed for many years in a variety of uses: in the construction of cars, packaging, telecommunications, etc.

Government consumption

The term government consumption refers to the services provided for consumers by the government (e.g. medical services, education, the maintenance of law and order). Economic growth allows an increase in government consumption. Indeed, a characteristic of the economic development of many countries has been an increase in the absolute and relative importance of this form of spending.

Composition of investment

We have seen that investment is an important 'engine' of economic growth. In turn economic growth permits additional choices to be made within investment. New types of plant and equipment are introduced, for use in the production of either new or existing products.

Economic growth may also permit additional spending on social capital: roads, hospitals, schools, libraries, leisure centres, and so on. Much of this spending is undertaken by the government at central or local level. (This capital yields the flow of services that we considered under the heading of government consumption.)

The arguments for and against government spending have been presented in detail in earlier chapters. It is sufficient to note here that governments have sometimes failed to make the best of the opportunities presented by economic growth. For instance, a priority in a number of less developed countries has been the development for the purposes of national prestige of a national airline, despite the fact that these airlines have usually incurred losses.

Other government expenditure

If economic growth is accompanied by an increase in national income per head of the working population, this allows the government to increase its tax revenue without an increase in tax rates. This increased revenue can then be used to finance other forms of government expenditure not considered above, such as retirement pensions, sickness and unemployment benefit.

> **Qu. 13.6** Explain the statement that changes in the pattern of expenditure are an important aspect of economic growth.

Leisure

One of the main benefits of economic growth is that it allows people to enjoy more leisure. A study of long-term trends in the UK suggests that about two-thirds of the *potential* increase in output has taken the form of the production of additional goods and services, and the remaining one-third an increase in leisure. This increase in leisure has been made up of a shorter working life (later start, earlier retirement), a shorter working week, and longer holidays. On the other hand there has been an increase in the proportion of women of working age taking paid employment.

Costs of economic growth

The production process gives rise to an output not only of goods and services but also of economic 'bads'. These bads include the pollution of rivers, lakes and the sea, increased noise, the release of smoke and chemicals into the atmosphere, increased injuries and deaths from road accidents and a loss of green spaces and other rural amenities.

A continual increase in all of these bads is not inevitable. Indeed, the UK has in recent years seen a reduction in the discharge of smoke, some improvements in the health of rivers and a slight decline in deaths from road accidents. But these improvements have occurred only because of government intervention, and the authorities must constantly be aware that economic growth can have costs as well as benefits.

> **Qu. 13.7** Why may economic growth not make everyone better off?

Economic growth and economic development

We noted earlier that economic growth is required for, but does not guarantee, economic development. Economic development implies not only an increase in income per head, but also a satisfactory form or direction of economic growth. Four factors are especially important:

Distribution of income and wealth
National income per head in the poorest countries such as India, Bangladesh, and countries in sub-Saharan Africa is less than $300, as compared to around $15 000 in Switzerland and Sweden. The vast majority of the population in these countries live in abject material poverty with an insufficiency of the basic necessities: food, clothing and shelter. Consequently an important test of these countries' economic development is the changes that occur in the consumption levels of the very poor.

Death rate

Another aspect of poverty is a high death rate. The infant mortality rate in Bangladesh, Algeria and Indonesia is ten times as high as in the UK, the USA and Japan. Life expectancy at birth in India is two-thirds of that in the UK and the USA.

Literacy

Illiteracy is widespread in poor countries. It is estimated that less than half the adult population in India, Nigeria, and Ethiopia can read and write. An improvement in literacy is seen as an important aspect of economic development.

Employment

There is a huge labour surplus in many less developed countries (LDCs). This manifests itself not so much as heavy unemployment as in widespread *underemployment.* Since the unemployed do not receive social security benefits, they are willing to take up any form of work in order to sustain themselves. Common occupations include the collecting and recycling of rubbish, very small scale trading, and personal services such as carrying the luggage of richer people.

> **Qu. 13.8** Distinguish between economic growth and economic development.

Strategies for development

Governments have adopted various strategies for development. Three main approaches can be identified, and these are considered below.

The development of agriculture

The LDCs have succeeded in increasing the output of many crops by means of the increased use of fertilisers, improved irrigation and drainage, and better seeds. This has allowed domestic consumption to increase. Unfortunately however, it has not contributed to another objective, an increase in export earnings, since it has been possible to sell the higher output on world markets only at lower prices. The World Bank has estimated that the real prices of agricultural products fell by a quarter between the 1950s and the 1970s. Moreover the downtrend in price has been accompanied by substantial price fluctuations. These factors have led to more attention being given to industrialisation.

Development through industrialisation

Between 1960 and 1980 the proportion of the labour force in

industry in the low income economies increased from 9 to 13 per cent, an indication of a desire for a greater measure of economic independence. A broad distinction can be made between two forms of development based on industrialisation:

1 *Import-substituting industrialisation* This strategy, which has been adopted by the majority of LDCs, has usually involved the establishment of large scale, capital-intensive, urban-based industries. These industries have frequently been protected by high tariff and other barriers (see Chapter 14), and usually supply goods to meet the needs of the middle and upper income groups.

This strategy has been extensively criticised on the ground that the high level of protection contravenes the principle of comparative advantage, leading to a misallocation of resources and the development of an inefficient industrial sector. This does not apply to the second form of development based on industrialisation.

2 *Export-led industrialisation* As the term suggests, this strategy is based on the development of industries to supply overseas markets. This strategy has been adopted by most of the newly industrialising countries that have achieved very high growth rates. For example, South Korea and Hong Kong, whose exports of manufactures account for around 90 per cent of their total exports, achieved a growth in real national income of around 10 per cent a year in the 1970s (about three times the growth rate achieved by European countries).

> **Qu. 13.9** Critically examine alternative strategies for economic development.

Intermediate technology

The policy of many LDCs, especially those adopting an import-substituting strategy, has also been criticised as relying on an inappropriate type of technology. Much of the plant required for mass production has to be purchased from, and often serviced by, the rich industrialised nations. Moreover, the number of jobs created is less than if a simpler 'intermediate' technology is used.

An example of this simpler technology is the development by the Intermediate Technology Group of a machine costing £30 000 that can make up to 12 000 glass bottles a day for medical, cosmetic and other consumer products. Automatic machines used in developed countries cost ten times as much and can produce up to several hundred thousand containers a day, far more than required by most developing countries. Moreover, the machines are extremely complex and need highly skilled personnel to maintain and operate them.

14

The International Economy

Introduction

In the previous two chapters our focus was on the national economy. We showed how an economy can grow and develop, and we examined some of the implications of growth.

In this chapter we widen our focus and consider various aspects of the international economy. In explaining the pattern of the international economy, we refer again to two factors that we have already discussed: differences in resource endowments, and the principle of comparative advantage.

Differences in resource endowments

No one who has been in more than one country can fail to notice that different countries are endowed with different resources. At the broadest level, agriculture flourishes more in some countries than others because of differences in soil and climate. Manufacturing is more important in some countries than others (e.g. in the USA as compared to Greece), because of differences in deposits of minerals, in labour force skills, etc.

Closer examination reveals further differences, further degrees of specialisation. Italy is known as a producer of fashion knitwear and leather goods, Japan and other Far Eastern countries as producers of domestic electrical appliances, Scotland as a producer of whisky. As countries specialise in those goods and services in which they have a *comparative advantage*, aggregate or international welfare increases.

Comparative advantage

It would be useful at this point to refresh your memory about the principle of comparative advantage by re-reading the relevant

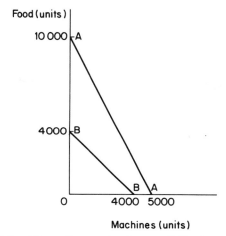

Fig. 14.1 Alternative production possibility boundaries

sections of Chapter 2. In that chapter the principle is applied to the activities of two individuals. In this chapter we apply it to two countries.

Figure 14.1 presents production possibility boundaries for two countries A and B. (The boundaries are drawn as straight lines to simplify the analysis.) If we assume that both countries have the same quantity of resources, it is clear that A has an *absolute advantage* in the production of food *and* machines. However, while A can produce 2½ times as much food as B, it can produce only 1¼ times as many machines. In other words A has a *comparative advantage* in the production of food, while B has a comparative advantage in the production of machines.

		Food	Machines
Country	A	5000	2500
	B	2000	2000
Total		7000	4500

The table above shows what output would be in the absence of specialisation, i.e. if each country devoted half its resources to the production of food and half to machines.

The table below shows what output would be if A devoted three-quarters of its resources to the production of food and one-quarter to machines, while B specialised entirely on machines. It can be seen that the output of both food and machines would be higher than in the previous situation.

		Food	Machines
Country	A	7500	1250
	B	–	4000
Total		7500	5250

Qu. 14.1 How does the principle of comparative advantage help to explain international specialisation and trade?

Qu. 14.2 Using a numerical example, explain the difference between absolute and comparative advantage.

Exchange

Countries will be willing to specialise only if a mechanism exists whereby they can exchange goods and services. Imagine the plight of country B if it could not exchange machines for food.

We saw in Chapter 3 that the most efficient method of exchange requires the use of money. In a domestic economy the money used is, of course, the national currency. Two things are required for efficient *international* exchange and trade:

1   Agreement on the rate at which domestic currencies exchange. We shall see below that this 'agreement' on exchange rates is sometimes reached by the governments of the countries concerned. But in most instances the exchange rate results from the operation of market forces.

2   An exchange rate between international price ratios. Whatever the form of the agreement, international exchange (and therefore specialisation) will not take place unless the exchange rate lies between the limits set by the international price ratios. To explain this we consider again the situation facing countries A and B in Figure 14.1.

Country A can produce 2 units of food for every machine. In other words it costs half as much to produce one unit of food as one machine. Relative costs are usually reflected in relative prices. So we might find, for example, that food costs $2 per unit and machines $4 each.

Country B can produce 1 unit of food for each machine. The relative costs of production, and hence relative prices, are equal. For example each unit of food and each machine might cost £1.

Applying the rule for international trade, the exchange rate would have to lie between the limits £1 = $2 (the price ratio for food) and £1 = $4 (the price ratio for machines). This is illustrated in the table below in which the domestic prices are given in the first row, and import prices at various exchange rates in the other rows.

Alternative Exchange Rates and International Trade

	A		B	
	Food	Machines	Food	Machines
Domestic prices	$2	$4	£1	£1
Import prices at exchange rate:				
£1 = $3	$3	$3	£0·67	£1·33
£1 = $5	$5	$5	£0·40	£0·80
£1 = $1	$1	$1	£2·00	£4·00

Of the three exchange rates only one, £1 = $3, falls between the price ratios £1 = $2 and £1 = $4. At this exchange rate producers in country A would be able to sell food in B, since they are happy to sell at a price of 67 pence a unit as compared to the price of £1 that would be charged by B's producers. A's producers are willing to sell at 67 pence since at an exchange rate of £1 = $3, 67 pence equals approximately $2, the price at which they sell food in the domestic market. (This assumes that no additional costs, e.g. for transport, are incurred in supplying country B.)

$$0·67 \times 3 = 2$$

Similarly B's producers are able to sell machines in country A. They sell at a price of $3 as compared to a price of $4 charged by A's producers. This $3 is equal to the £1 per machine that B's producers obtain in the domestic market.

$$3 \times \tfrac{1}{3} = 1$$

We see then that international trade would take place at an exchange rate of £1 = $3. A would supply food to B, and B would supply machines to A. However, international trade would *not* occur at the other two exchange rates listed in the table above, since they lie outside the international price ratios.

If the exchange rate was £1 = $5 A's producers would be happy to supply both food and machines to B. However, B's producers would be unable to sell either food or machines in A because their prices would be above the domestic prices. B would therefore be unable to earn the dollars with which to pay for its imports from A. An offer to pay with pounds would not be accepted, since the pounds could not be put to use (A does not buy anything from B).

The same problem would arise at an exchange rate of £1 = $1. In this instance B would be able to sell food and machines in A, but A would not be able to sell anything in B.

Multilateral trade

The above situation is one of *bilateral trade*, where each country trades with only one other country. In practice international trade is *multilateral*, with each country trading with very many others.

This *may* mean that the problem that we identified above becomes less serious. Country A might be willing to sell food and machines to B and to accept payment in pounds, if those pounds could be used to pay for goods imported by A from other countries. For its part B might be satisfied with this arrangement provided that it could sell machines to other countries.

However, the principle illustrated in the table remains of the utmost importance. The prices of one country's goods and services, relative to those of other countries, must be reflected in that country's exchange rates. Otherwise the country will experience a serious imbalance on its international trade, having either a substantial surplus of exports over imports, or of imports over exports. In fact the existence of a substantial *trade gap* will usually cause the exchange rate to move to a more appropriate level, as explained in the following section.

> **Qu. 14.3**   What conditions must be fulfilled for international trade to take place?

Determination of the exchange rate

In this section we consider how exchange rates are determined by the interplay of market forces. We subsequently discuss government intervention to modify the operation of market forces. We take as our example the rate of exchange between the pound sterling and the US dollar.

Figure 14.2 presents demand and supply curves for sterling. The price of sterling is given in terms of the number of dollars per pound. So, for example, sterling would be expensive at an exchange rate of £1 = $3, and cheap at a rate of £1 = $1.

The demand and supply curves have the usual shapes, although the supply curve could in fact have other shapes. (To explain this would require more advanced analysis than would be appropriate.)

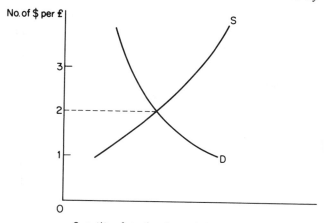

Fig. 14.2 Equilibrium rate of exchange

Given these demand and supply curves the equilibrium rate of exchange is £1 = $2. At this rate the value of exports is assumed to equal the value of imports.

An increase in exports

Let us now see what would happen if a favourable trade gap appeared because the value of UK exports increased, imports

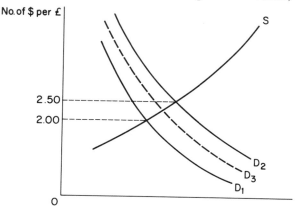

Fig. 14.3 Increase in exports and rise in exchange rate

remaining unchanged. In order to buy more British goods, importers would require more sterling. This is represented by the shift of the demand curve from D_1 to D_2 in Figure 14.3.

As a result of the increased demand for sterling the rate of exchange moves to £1 = $2·50, i.e. sterling has become more expensive. The result of the change in the price of sterling is that the disequilibrium in trade will be corrected; the trade gap will become smaller and should eventually disappear.

Disequilibrium corrected
In order to understand why this is so consider a British manufacturer of bicycles which sell on the domestic or home market for £100. At the initial exchange rate of £1 = $2 he sells bicycles in the USA for $200 (this ignores any additional costs of selling abroad). But when the exchange rate rises to £1 = $2·50 he needs to sell at $250 in order to obtain £100. At this higher price the manufacturer sells fewer bicycles; consequently the demand for sterling falls to D_3 (Figure 14.3). For example if he sold 5000 as compared to 6000 bikes, importers would demand £500 000 as compared to £600 000.

An increase in imports
An unfavourable trade gap would result from an increase in imports, exports remaining unchanged. In Figure 14.4 the initial equilibrium rate of exchange is £1 = $2. UK importers then increase

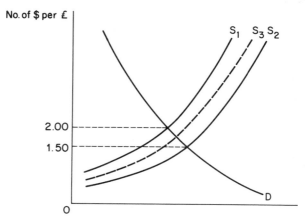

Fig. 14.4   Increase in imports and fall in exchange rate

their purchases of US goods. In order to pay for these imports they need more dollars. They therefore bring more sterling to the market to exchange for dollars. This is shown in Figure 14.4 by a shift of the supply curve from S_1 to S_2. This causes the exchange rate to fall from £1 = $2 to £1 = $1·50.

Disequilibrium corrected

To understand how the fall in the exchange rate helps to correct the trade disequilibrium, consider a US manufacturer of writing sets which sell in the USA for $9. At the initial exchange rate of £1 = $2, the manufacturer sells in the UK at £4·50. But after the exchange rate falls to £1 = $1·50 the firm has to sell at £6, since this is now the equivalent of $9. At the higher price fewer sets are bought, and the supply of sterling (to be exchanged for dollars) falls to S_3 (Figure 14.4).

Qu. 14.4 Define the equilibrium exchange rate and discuss the factors that would cause the equilibrium rate to change.

Qu. 14.5 Show how (a) a trade gap is likely to affect the exchange rate, (b) a change in the exchange rate is likely to affect the trade gap.

Government intervention

So far we have assumed that the exchange rate is allowed to *float* in response to changes in demand and supply. But governments are often unwilling to allow exchange rates to float freely. Governments intervene from time to time in order to smooth out fluctuations in exchange rates, a system known as *dirty floating*. In other instances governments 'peg' or fix the exchange rate.

Fixed exchange rate

The main advantage of fixed exchange rates are:

1 *Greater certainty in international transactions* When exporters and importers enter into contracts, payment may not be made for several months ahead. If they know that the exchange rate will not change, they have a much better idea about the price of the contract in terms of their own currency.

2 *Greater government influence over price* As we saw above, a change in the exchange rate can lead to a change in import prices. In industrialised economies it is not unusual for imports to account for about a quarter of the total expenditure of households and firms. Consequently a substantial change in import prices can have an appreciable effect on the overall price level, i.e. on the cost of living.

By fixing the exchange rate, one source of price fluctuations is avoided.

Disadvantages of fixed exchange rates

The main disadvantage of fixed exchange rates can be explained by reference to Figure 14.5. The rate of exchange has been fixed at £1 = $2, but because of a trade deficit, the underlying equilibrium rate of exchange – the rate that would result from the operation of market forces – is £1 = $1·50.

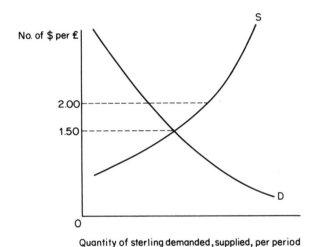

Fig. 14.5   Disequilibrium rate of exchange

At a price of $2 more sterling is supplied to the market than is demanded. In order to sustain this price the authorities (in the UK the Bank of England acting in conjunction with the Treasury) have to 'purchase' the excess supply. They do so by supplying other currencies, in this instance dollars, in exchange for sterling.

The danger of this policy is that the authorities may eventually run out of foreign exchange. This would lead to a loss of confidence in sterling that would be extremely serious and to a disruption of the UK's international economic relationships. In order to prevent this happening, the authorities may resort to (*a*) *deflation* or (*b*) *devaluation*.

Deflation

The term deflation denotes that as a result of government policy aggregate demand is less than it would otherwise be. As the level of imports falls, in response to the lower demand, the supply of sterling falls from S_1 to S_2 in Figure 14.6. The equilibrium rate of exchange rises from £1 = $1·50 to £1 = $2, i.e. it comes into line with the official rate. Sterling is no longer in excess supply.

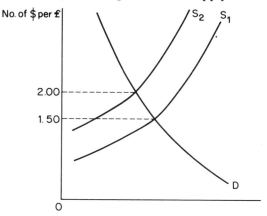

Fig. 14.6   Deflation and the rate of exchange

The disadvantage of deflation is, of course, that demand falls for the output of domestic producers as well as for imports. Consequently domestic income and employment fall. Given these disadvantages the government may prefer to devalue the currency rather than deflate the economy.

Devaluation

When a currency is devalued the authorities fix a new, lower value. Since devaluations are usually a response to a substantial excess supply of the currency concerned, the change in the exchange rate is also usually substantial – frequently more than 10 per cent.

Revaluation

When the situation is the reverse of that described above, i.e. when there is an excess *demand* for a currency, the authorities may choose a new, higher rate of exchange. This is usually termed *revaluation*. But some people prefer the term *upvaluation*, using revaluation to cover both devaluation and upvaluation.

Qu. 14.6 Discuss the advantages and disadvantages of a fixed exchange rate.

Qu. 14.7 Evaluate the relative merits of deflation and devaluation as responses to a balance of payments deficit.

Balance of payments

A country's balance of payments is a summary of all the international transactions that involve financial flows. The table below presents a balance of payments table for an imaginary country. For each item the figure recorded is the financial inflow minus the corresponding financial outflow. For example exports of goods give rise to a financial inflow, imports to a financial outflow; a simplified balance of these two flows is illustrated in the table below.

Visible balance	−100
Invisible balance	+200
Current balance	+100
Investment and other capital transactions	− 50
Balance for official financing	+ 50
Additions to reserves	− 50

The *visible balance* refers to all trade in goods: food, raw materials, manufactures etc. Our imaginary country imported a higher value of goods than it exported, i.e. it had a deficit on visible trade of 100.

On the other hand there was a surplus on *invisible trade* of 200. The invisible balance includes payments for:

(a) services, e.g. insurance, shipping, tourism;
(b) transfers, e.g. military and economic assistance;
(c) interest, profits and dividends.

Adding together the visible and invisible balances gives the *current balance* which showed a surplus of 100. The current balance indicates whether or not a country is paying its way on a day-to-day basis. If a country has a substantial deficit on its current account, this may well indicate that its industry has become uncompetitive.

Consequently a great deal of importance is attached to the current balance. Indeed in popular newspapers the term balance of payments is sometimes applied to the current balance (and even to the visible balance). However, this is incorrect since it ignores the remaining flows in the balance of payments account.

Investment and other capital transactions are of three broad types:

(a) Overseas investment in the private sector, e.g. purchases of shares in existing subsidiaries or expenditure to establish new subsidiary companies.

(*b*) Deposits with banks and other financial institutions.

(*c*) Purchases of securities issued by central and local government.

Our imaginary country had a deficit on investment and capital transactions of 50, i.e. it invested 50 more overseas than was invested here by overseas institutions and individuals. This outflow of money would be expected to give rise to inflows in subsequent years especially in the form of interest, profits and dividends. As we have seen these are part of the invisible, and hence the current, balance.

These transactions sometimes give rise to considerable controversy. On the one hand it is argued that firms should be persuaded (or even forced) to invest at home rather than overseas, in order to create employment at home. On the other hand it is argued that foreign investment in this country should be discouraged because it means that in future years profits will flow out of the country. The fact that these two arguments are inconsistent has not always prevented them both from being advanced by the same people!

Adding together all the above flows gives a *balance for official financing* of 50, i.e. there was an overall surplus of 50. This surplus allowed 50 to be added to the country's *currency reserves*. (This is included in the table on p. 158 as − 50 in order to balance the +50 on the balance for official financing. This is an accounting convention and helps to explain why it is said that 'the balance of payments must always balance'.)

Balance of payments and the exchange rate

In an earlier section we discussed the interaction between trade in goods and services and the exchange rate. A similar interaction exists between capital flows and the exchange rate, and indeed between the sum of current and capital flows and the exchange rate.

> **Qu. 14.8** 'Since the balance of payments must always balance, it need never be a source of concern.' Discuss.

Barriers to trade

We began this chapter by considering the advantages of international specialisation and trade. To conclude we examine the barriers that prevent or inhibit international trade. A broad distinction can be made between *natural* and *artificial* barriers.

Natural barriers

There are three main natural barriers to international trade:

1   *Additional costs of selling in overseas markets*   In our earlier examples we assumed that no additional costs were incurred in selling in overseas markets. In practice, however, there are usually some additional costs, the most widespread being *transport* costs. Transport costs are especially important in relation to heavy or bulky low-price items, such as bricks. They are much less important for smaller, expensive items such as jewellery.

In recent years technological changes have reduced the importance of transport costs. These changes include: containerisation, the introduction of large freight aircraft, and developments in telecommunications.

2   *Imperfect information*   Information may be imperfect on the part of suppliers and purchasers. *Suppliers* may simply be unaware of the opportunities that exist for profitable international trade. Recognising this, many governments subsidise in various ways the cost of acquiring information: by establishing commercial units in overseas embassies, by financial assistance to trade missions and exhibitions, and by the provision of market information and data. *Buyers* may be unaware of the existence of the goods and services provided by overseas suppliers. Suppliers attempt to overcome this by advertising, and some of the government measures discussed in the previous section may also help in this respect.

3   *Set-up costs*   Initial set-up costs are incurred whenever a firm attempts to penetrate a new market, and these costs may be especially high with regard to overseas markets. For example the firm may need to build new warehouses, and to recruit a new sales staff. It may need to spend time and money familiarising itself with local customs and requirements. Moreover to meet local requirements it is sometimes necessary to re-design products. Finally it may be necessary to spend more on advertising a product when it is first introduced to a market than when it has become established.

Set-up costs may prevent firms from entering overseas markets, even though once established their costs would be no higher than those of domestic suppliers. This barrier can be especially important for small firms. They are often less able to bear the risks of incurring set-up costs without any guarantee of subsequent success.

Artificial barriers to trade

Artificial barriers to trade are mainly the result of government intervention in the operation of market forces. They can be classified under three headings:

Tariffs

Tariffs are taxes imposed on imports. They can be levied on an *ad valorem* basis, i.e. as a certain percentage of price (value), or on a specific basis, i.e. as a given amount per unit. By increasing the price of the product, a tariff reduces the quantity demanded.

Quotas

Quotas are quantitative restrictions on imports. A quota may relate to the total quantity or value of a commodity that can be imported in a given period. Alternatively it may relate to the quantity or value that can be imported from a particular source, e.g. from a certain country or group of countries.

Other barriers to trade

The post-war period has seen a substantial reduction in the overall level of tariffs. On the other hand there has been an increase in other barriers to trade. These include administrative procedures – technical standards, marks of origin (e.g. made in Japan), environmental controls, customs valuation procedures – which often put foreign suppliers at a disadvantage. For example Jaguar, the British car manufacturer, had to modify the exhaust system of a new model to satisfy the requirements of the US market. France insisted for a while that all imported video recorders had to be registered at a small customs post in a remote location, seriously disrupting imports from Japan. The Japanese themselves have often been accused of insisting on testing procedures, e.g. for domestic electrical appliances, that are especially burdensome for foreign suppliers.

Government purchasing policies often favour domestic producers, sometimes to the complete exclusion of foreign competitors. For example UK governments have usually bought British computers. Financial aid may be given to overseas countries on condition that some or all of it is spent on imports from the donor country; this obviously puts other producers at a disadvantage. Exchange controls, most commonly imposed by less developed countries, often operate to restrict imports.

> **Qu. 14.9** Using demand and supply diagrams, compare and contrast the impact of tariffs and quotas.

Voluntary export restraints

A voluntary export restraint is an agreement between two parties (government or industries) whereby one country agrees to restrict the volume of its exports to the other country. Although the agreement is entered into voluntarily, it often reflects a fear by the exporter that a compulsory restriction might otherwise be imposed. So, for example, Japanese car manufacturers limit their exports to the UK to avoid the danger that the UK government might impose a quota.

Effects of trade barriers

The most obvious effect is, of course, that the level of international trade is less than it would otherwise be. Following from this, less advantage is taken of the benefits of international specialisation.

In addition there are several other effects at the national level:

Higher prices
Prices may rise for several reasons:

(*a*)   When tariffs are imposed the prices of imported goods rise.
(*b*)   Higher import prices act as an 'umbrella', allowing domestic producers to put up their prices.
(*c*)   If tariffs are imposed on raw materials and components this causes increases in the costs, and hence the prices, of domestic products.
(*d*)   Price is likely to rise when any barrier, e.g. a quota, restricts supply, for the reasons explained in Chapter 6.

Restriction of consumer choice
This occurs as a result of the introduction of quotas, voluntary export restraints or any other measure that discourages or restricts imports.

Employment
Employment in exporting countries is obviously reduced by any measures to restrict imports. The effect on employment in the importing country is less easy to predict, since there are conflicting tendencies:

(*a*)   Increased output by domestic producers in the protected markets requires extra workers.
(*b*)   Higher prices in the protected markets causes a fall in the real income of consumers. This fall in income causes a fall in expenditure, and hence in output and employment, in other markets.
(*c*)   Overseas suppliers may establish production facilities and hence provide employment in countries which restrict imports. (See the section on multinational companies in Chapter 8.)

Efficiency

The basic purpose of barriers to trade is to protect less efficient firms from more efficient competitors. In general, therefore, the effect of barriers is to reduce the overall level of efficiency. However, there are two possible exceptions to this rule:

1 *Infant industries* When an industry is first established in a country its costs may be higher than in other countries where the industry is long-established. These higher costs result from a lack of experience. (We showed above how learning and experience can result in a fall in costs.) It is argued that these industries should be given temporary protection. As they mature it is possible to remove the protective barriers; market forces will then ensure that specialisation and trade take place in accordance with the principle of comparative advantage. This argument has a strong appeal, especially when the infant industry is located in a less developed country with a low national income. However, in practice infant industries often take much longer to reach maturity than was initially envisaged, and 'temporary' barriers have a habit of becoming permanent.

2 *Re-organisation of an industry* Similar reasoning is advanced here. However, it is usually applied when the markets of a long-established industry are under attack from younger competitors. It is argued that if the industry is protected, it will be 'slimmed down' in an orderly manner; planning will ensure that capacity is reduced to an appropriate level. Then the protection can be removed. Again, however, in practice protection is often maintained for a longer period than was initially envisaged.

> **Qu. 14.10** Discuss the effect of trade barriers on economic welfare.

15

International Economic Institutions

The institutions that we discuss in this chapter have three major objectives (different objectives being important for different institutions). These objectives are:

1   To facilitate the expansion of international trade by:

(a)   reducing barriers to trade;
(b)   increasing world liquidity;
(c)   providing assistance to countries facing balance of payments difficulties, so that these countries do not need to restrict trade.

2   To aid the economic development of less developed countries (LDCs).

3   To increase living standards. There is an overlap here with the other two objectives, since the expansion of international trade and economic development are both associated with an increase in living standards. But some countries have adopted additional measures to increase their own living standards by establishing trading groups, e.g. the European Economic Community. The operations of these groups are examined towards the end of the chapter. We begin by discussing an institution whose objective is the reduction of barriers to trade.

General Agreement on Tariffs and Trade (GATT)

The advantages to be derived from international specialisation and trade were the main reason for the establishment in 1947 of the General Agreement on Tariffs and Trade, an international organisation whose headquarters are in Switzerland. The members of GATT are pledged to the expansion of multilateral trade, and to a reduction of measures which distort the pattern of trade such as import restrictions and export incentives.

GATT has sponsored seven rounds of negotiations which have resulted in the average import *tariffs* of the industrialised nations being reduced from about 40 per cent to less than 10 per cent. This has aided trade among the industrialised nations, and has helped to widen the markets for the products of the less developed countries. Unfortunately some other forms of barriers to trade have increased in extent, as noted in Chapter 14.

The LDCs enjoy concessions under GATT rules, including exemption from tariffs on certain of their exports, and the right to control imports when they run into balance of payments difficulties. These departures from the usual GATT principle of non-discrimination in trade policy were justified by the need to aid the development and raise the living standards of the LDCs.

International Monetary Fund (IMF)

The IMF was established in 1945 and now has 146 members. The Fund's resources are provided by members according to a system of quotas related to the size of their economies. Seventy-five per cent of the quota is paid in the member's own currency and 25 per cent in other currencies ('reserve assets'). The Fund also issues Special Drawing Rights. SDRs are in effect entries in members' bank balances with the IMF, and are available for settlement between central banks and with the IMF.

Until recently the main use of IMF funds was to help countries to meet temporary balance of payments difficulties. These funds reduce the need to restrict imports or *substantially* deflate the economy (e.g. by increasing taxation). However, before funds are made available the IMF requires assurances that the country concerned will take steps to remedy any persistent weakness on the balance of payments, and these steps might include reducing expenditure.

In recent years short-term assistance has become less important as countries have increasingly met their need for temporary finance by borrowing from commercial banks without submitting to the policy conditions imposed by the IMF. The Fund has responded by offering assistance for longer periods and with less strict conditions. This has brought the IMF closer to the activities of the World Bank (see below).

Another important function of the IMF has been as *mediator* in negotiations between LDCs which have experienced difficulties in repaying loans and the banks from which they have borrowed. For example, Mexico borrowed heavily on the security of future oil revenues, but was unable to repay when the price of oil slumped. The banks were reluctant to shoulder all the risks of renewing or re-scheduling the loans, and the arrangements agreed in this and similar instances had three ingredients:

(a) The commercial banks agreed to re-schedule the outstanding debt, and to increase their lending.
(b) This lending was supplemented by finance from the IMF.
(c) The IMF's contribution was conditional on the borrower adopting an austerity programme.

All three ingredients were required for an agreement to be concluded. The banks would not agree without the participation of the IMF.

By 1984 the IMF was supporting adjustment programmes in forty countries, and had to call on its members to increase their subscriptions.

Despite the increased assistance that it has provided, the activities of the IMF have been criticised as inadequate by some Third World countries. These countries have argued that they should receive a larger share of the Fund's resources. Moreover they wish to see a lengthening of the period for which assistance is provided, an easing of the conditions on which money is loaned, and subsidies to reduce the interest cost for poor countries borrowing from the Fund.

The cost of these policy changes would, of course, have to be met by the Fund's richer members. This is, therefore, part of the wider debate about the distribution of the world's wealth.

The International Bank for Reconstruction and Development (IBRD)

The IBRD was established at the same time as the IMF and has virtually the same membership. It is popularly known as the *World Bank*, a title used by the IBRD itself to describe collectively the Bank and the International Development Association (see below).

Capital subscriptions to the Bank are related to the wealth of its member states, but the Bank obtains most of its funds by borrowing on world markets. Consequently it charges market-related rates of interest on its loans. However, because of its size and status the Bank can borrow at lower rates than could the countries to which it makes loans, and this benefit is passed on to borrowers.

Loans are made either to governments or under government guarantee for a wide range of development and welfare purposes, almost entirely to LDCs. The Bank also provides various kinds of technical assistance. Long-term funding of specific projects accounts for 90 per cent of the Bank's total lending. Recently it has also provided assistance, not tied to specific projects, for the support of development programmes in countries with short-term foreign exchange problems. (This has contributed to the overlap between the activities of the Bank and of the IMF.)

Lending by the World Bank has risen rapidly in the 1980s, partly because it has introduced new forms of lending, and partly because it has begun to participate in joint operations with the commercial banks (another parallel with the IMF). The aims of this co-operation are:

(*a*) To provide assistance over longer periods than would normally be possible from private sector sources.
(*b*) By strengthening investors' confidence, to promote increased lending by the private sector.

The stimulation of aid from private sector sources to the LDCs is the main aim of the *International Finance Corporation*, an affiliate of the IBRD. In addition to providing loans, the IFC can hold shares in companies. Also affiliated to the IBRD, the *International Development Association* provides loans at little or no interest for projects in developing countries that would not be feasible if money had to be borrowed at normal commercial rates. These projects are capital intensive and often have a long life, e.g. road building, or the construction of an electricity distribution network.

> **Qu. 15.1** What policies may aid the expansion of international trade?
> **Qu. 15.2** Outline the main objectives of the following institutions: (*a*) GATT, (*b*) IMF, (*c*) World Bank.

Bank for International Settlements

The main purpose of the BIS is to promote central bank co-operation, including the provision of short-term liquidity to central banks in need. The BIS has played an important role in providing temporary finance to countries with liquidity problems. For example it made 'bridging loans' of $925 millions to Mexico, and $1·45 billion to Brazil, while these countries were negotiating credits from the IMF.

The contribution of international economic institutions

Despite the expansion that has occurred in the activities of these international economic institutions, grave problems remain.

Moreover it seems that the contribution of these institutions is bound to be limited, for the reasons outlined in the following sections.

World liquidity

Despite numerous increases since its establishment, IMF credits and SDRs account for less than a tenth of *world official reserves*, the bulk of which comprise foreign currencies (the most important being the dollar) and gold. Moreover, IMF funds account for an even smaller proportion of *total world liquidity* which includes various 'arrangements to lend', made between one country and another. (These arrangements are similar to the provision of an overdraft facility that is only used as and when required.)

As noted in the introduction to this chapter, an increase in world liquidity helps to finance an expansion in international trade. There is no evidence that a *general* shortage of liquidity has inhibited trade. However, some developing countries have suffered extreme liquidity problems, as noted above.

Economic development

We noted in Chapter 13 some of the inequalities that exist as between the developed and the less developed countries. The World Bank has estimated that 5 per cent of the world's output is shared by the 47 per cent of the population who live in low income countries such as Bangladesh, China, India, Pakistan and countries in sub-Saharan Africa.

Foreign assistance and economic development

It is easy to demonstrate how *in principle* foreign assistance can contribute to economic development. As we showed in Chapter 13, a country that wishes to increase the resources devoted to the production of capital goods may have to temporarily reduce its output of consumption goods. This reduction in output may cause severe hardship, and even loss of life, if consumption is already close to the subsistence level. Foreign assistance can help to avoid this dilemma by making funds available for the purchase of the capital equipment required for economic development.

Sources of assistance

A broad distinction can be made between two forms of assistance: *economic aid* and *non-concessional assistance*.

Economic aid

Economic aid represents about 40 per cent of total assistance, and comprises:

1 *Official Development Assistance (ODA)* Around 80 per cent of ODA is bilateral, i.e. it is supplied directly by one country to another. The remaining 20 per cent is supplied by the various multilateral agencies discussed in previous sections. Although the share of these agencies has been increasing, it is still relatively small. However, the provision of aid by these agencies can help to unlock other sources of finance, as noted above. The United Nations has set a target for its members, that 0·7 per cent of their national income should be given as ODA. Although some countries, e.g. Norway and the Netherlands, exceed this figure, most fall short, e.g. the UK's contribution is only about half the target amount.

2 *Grants by voluntary agencies* This is the form of assistance that is best known to the general public. It includes the aid provided by such long-established institutions as Oxfam and Tearfund, and a number of individual campaigns. Although the money raised by these agencies can be of immense importance to the recipients, voluntary aid accounts for only 5 per cent of economic aid and 2 per cent of total economic assistance.

Non-concessional assistance

Assistance provided at non-concessional (commercial) rates has increased in relative importance, and now accounts for about 60 per cent of total assistance.

International debt

As noted above, foreign assistance can be used to purchase plant and equipment in order to build up a country's economic capacity. If the assistance takes the form of a loan, and not a grant, it involves subsequent outflows of funds in the form of interest payments and, eventually, the repayment of the loan.

In the 1970s and early 1980s the increase in oil prices caused large balance of payments deficits for many LDCs. To meet these deficits they further increased their external debt, and the financing of this debt became increasingly onerous. The World Bank estimated that by the mid-1980s the external debt of developing countries without oil reserves amounted to more than one-third of their national income, and that around one-quarter of their export earnings would have been required to service the debt.

The case against economic aid

We explained above how economic aid (as part of economic assistance) can *in principle* aid the recipients. It is also argued that the donor countries obtain some benefits which help to offset the costs. One alleged benefit is greater international political stability. Another is the increased sales opportunities provided by higher incomes in the countries receiving aid.

It would seem then that the overall effect of economic aid must be beneficial. However, this conclusion is not accepted by all economists. Several arguments against the provision of economic aid have been advanced:

(*a*)   Economic aid is often used inefficiently, in projects that contribute more to the prestige than the development of the country (see Chapter 13).

(*b*)   Foreign funds are often used to replace, rather than supplement domestic funds.

These two arguments suggest that some of the potential benefits of economic aid may 'leak away'. This leakage could be seen as an acceptable price to pay for the benefits that do accrue, given the huge disparities in living standards that exist. However, two further arguments have been advanced which imply that the disadvantages of aid could outweigh the advantages:

(*c*)   Aid is sometimes used to help undemocratic governments to retain power.

(*d*)   The receipt of aid may sap local initiative, making the recipients even more dependent on the donors.

> **Qu. 15.3**   Present the arguments (*a*) for, (*b*) against, the provision of economic aid.

Trade and economic development

The evidence does not enable the debate to be resolved. The 'pro-aid' and 'anti-aid' schools can both point to particular instances that justify their views. However, there is a greater measure of agreement that policies should be adopted to promote the development of the LDCs through *increased trade*. These policies include:

(*a*)   Reducing barriers to trade and, where barriers are retained, giving preference to exports from LDCs. As we saw above, some progress has been made in this respect.

(*b*)   Reducing the proportion of aid that is tied, i.e. the recipient is required to spend a certain percentage (up to 100 per cent in extreme instances) in purchasing products from the donor country. It is estimated that about three quarters of UK bilateral trade is tied in this way.

Qu. 15.4 Explain how foreign assistance can contribute to a country's economic development.

Qu. 15.5 Comment on the UK's provision of Official Development Assistance in the light of the target set by the United Nations.

Regional trade groupings

In this section we discuss institutions whose objectives may include those discussed above but whose main objective is to increase their own economic welfare. There are two main forms of regional trade grouping: *free trade areas* and *customs unions*.

Free trade areas

In a free trade area all restrictions on trade between members are removed. But each member remains free to decide upon its policy in relation to non-members. An example is the Latin American Free Trade Area, which currently comprises ten South American countries.

Customs unions

As in a free trade area, in a customs union all restrictions on trade between members are abolished. Individual members also give up their right to decide upon their policies towards non-members. Instead a *common external tariff*, observed by all members, is established. Members may also adopt common policies in other spheres. The best known customs union is the European Economic Community (the Common Market), the major economic institution of the European Community.

Qu. 15.6 Show how a free trade area and a customs union (*a*) are alike, (*b*) differ.

European Economic Community (EEC)

The main objectives of the EEC are as follows:

1 *To increase specialisation and trade within the Community* The abolition of internal barriers to trade is the means of achieving this objective.

2   *To support the Community's agriculture industry*   Support is provided partly by grants intended to make the industry more efficient, e.g. by amalgamating small farms into larger units. But most support has been given under the Common Agricultural Policy by guaranteeing the prices at which farmers can sell their produce. Spending under this head accounts for almost two thirds of the EEC's total spending.

Such a high level of expenditure is mainly due to the fact that high prices have been set for a number of farm products. This has led to more being produced than could be sold within the Community, and thus to the build-up of stocks held by the Community (e.g. the infamous butter mountain and wine lake). These stocks have to be sold at prices well below those paid to farmers. For example, the cost in 1986 of disposing of stocks of beef and butter was estimated at £750 millions.

3   *To reduce inequalities within the Community*   Three institutions are especially important in this respect:

(a)   *European Investment Bank (EIB)* makes loans for projects that benefit less developed regions (two-thirds of the Bank's total spending); or cannot be financed by a single country; or are of common interest to several member countries (e.g. improving cross-border communications).

(b)   *European Regional Development Fund (ERDF)* was established to help correct regional imbalances in member countries. The UK has been one of the main beneficiaries of the Fund, mostly for projects in the Assisted Areas (areas of above-average unemployment).

(c)   *European Social Fund (ESF)* has the primary purpose of increasing workers' geographical and occupational mobility. It does this by assisting a number of projects, including training and re-training schemes; and schemes to improve the employment prospects of disadvantaged groups (e.g. disabled people).

An example of the assistance offered by the Fund was to meet the cost of re-training workers whose jobs in the newspaper industry were threatened by technological change.

The Community's revenue

In order to finance expenditure under these various heads the Community obtains revenue from three sources:

(a)   Duties levied on imports entering the Community under the Common External Tariff.

(*b*) Levies charged on agricultural products from outside the Community to bring their prices up to the levels prevailing under the Common Agricultural Policy price support regime.

(*c*) The yield of a Value Added Tax levied throughout the Community, the current rate being 1·4 per cent. This money is paid to the Community out of the VAT tax revenue of each member state.

Economic effects of a customs union

We can distinguish between the internal and external effects of a customs union.

Internal effects

There are two major internal effects:

(*a*) The removal of internal barriers to trade should increase overall efficiency and hence increase real national income.

(*b*) Other measures may lead to a redistribution of income. For example, some countries in the EEC are net beneficiaries (revenue exceeds contributions to the Community), while others are net contributors. There may also be a redistribution of income towards the poorer *regions* of the Community (e.g. Southern Italy).

External effects

If the common external tariff is higher than the individual tariffs that it replaces, international specialisation in accordance with the principle of comparative advantage will be reduced. For example, the UK sugar beet industry has expanded as imports from lower-cost producers of cane sugar have been excluded.

Furthermore surplus EEC sugar is sold outside the Community at subsidised prices. These sales drive down world prices, to the disadvantage of other sugar-producing nations, many of whom have very low incomes.

Despite preferential treatment for some poorer agricultural nations, it appears that the overall effect of the EEC's Common Agricultural Policy might well have been to redistribute income from poorer to richer nations. This is, of course, not an inevitable consequence of a customs union, but a result of the political processes that influence the conduct of the EEC.

16

Economic Performance

Introduction

In this chapter we seek to answer the question: how can we decide whether an economy is performing satisfactorily? We shall see that in order to answer this question we must:

(*a*)   Construct a list of *indicators* of performance.
(*b*)   Allocate relative *weights* to these indicators, i.e. decide which aspects of performance are more important and which are less important.

We begin by presenting a list of indicators, drawing on the analysis in previous chapters. These indicators are:
1   National income
2   Standard of living
3   Employment and unemployment
4   Rate of inflation
5   Balance of payments
6   Economic capacity
7   Equality

National income

As we saw in Chapter 12, national income can be measured in several ways, as a flow of output, of income or of expenditure. Total or aggregate expenditure is composed of spending on *consumption* goods, spending on *investment* goods, *government consumption*, and *exports minus imports*.

The *value* of expenditure in any given period is obtained by multiplying the *volume* of goods and services purchased by the *price* of these goods and services. This is illustrated by the data for an imaginary economy presented in the table below. In modern economies millions of transactions occur every year. Statisticians aggregate these transactions in the way shown in the table, although in real economies the numbers are, of course, very much bigger.

Nominal National Income

	Volume (units)	Price (£)	Value (£)
Consumption	1 000 000	10	10 000 000
Investment	10 000	200	2 000 000
Government consumption	100 000	20	2 000 000
Exports *minus* Imports	20 000	50	1 000 000
			15 000 000

Consumers buy one million units (e.g. food, haircuts, cars) at an average price of £10, giving a total value for consumption of £10 millions. Firms buy ten thousand units (e.g. machines, raw materials) at an average price of £200, giving a total value for investment of £2 millions.

Exports and imports comprise both consumption and investment goods. In this period our imaginary country's exports exceeded its imports by £1 million. Finally, government consumption amounted to £2 millions.

Note that the 'price' of £20 for government consumption is based on the *cost of supplying* the various items of government consumption, e.g. medical services are priced at the cost of the salaries of doctors, nurses, etc., *not* at the price charged to consumers. The reason for this is that medical services, and many other items of government consumption, are provided free ('zero price'). Using these prices would seriously underestimate the value of the services to the consumer.

Aggregating these expenditure flows gives us a figure of £15 millions. This is the nominal value of national income.

Nominal and real national income

Nominal national income can change because of a change in either the volume of purchases or their average price, or both. *Real* national income, on the other hand, changes only when the volume of purchases changes. The difference is illustrated in the table on page 176.

Changes in National Income

	Volume (units)	Price (£)	Value (£)	Index No. (base = 100)
Year 1 (base year)	1 000 000	100	100 000 000	100
Year 2	1 000 000	110	110 000 000	110
Year 3	1 100 000	100	110 000 000	110
Year 4	1 100 000	110	121 000 000	121

In year 1, with 1 million units purchased at an average price of £100, national income is £100 millions. Subsequent changes in national income are measured with respect to year 1, which is therefore called the *base year*.

In year 2 nominal national income is £110 millions, an increase of 10 per cent. Expressing this in index number form, with the base at 100, national income is 110. However, the increase in national income is entirely due to an increase in prices. The volume of purchases, i.e. real national income, is unchanged.

In year 3 nominal national income has again increased, with respect to year 1, by 10 per cent. The index is again 110. But in this instance, the increase is entirely due to the increase in the volume of purchases. Nominal and real income have both increased by 10 per cent.

In practice it is common for the volume of purchases *and* prices to increase over the course of a year. This situation is illustrated by the change between year 1 and year 4. Nominal national income increases by 21 per cent; the index is 121. This increase comprises a 10 per cent increase in volume and hence in real income, and a 10 per cent increase in price:

$$\frac{110}{100} \times \frac{110}{100} = \frac{121}{100}$$

Qu. 16.1   Explain the distinction between nominal and real national income and give a numerical example to show why they may not change to the same extent.

Standard of living

The term 'standard of living' is a layman's term rather than a technical economic term. It normally indicates the material well-being enjoyed by a country's citizens. There is obviously a close connection with national income, and the national income and the standard of living usually move in the same direction. However, the link between them is by no means automatic, as explained in the following section.

Composition of national income and the standard of living

The three aspects of the composition of the national income that can affect the standard of living are considered below.

Consumption versus investment

As we noted earlier, aggregate expenditure equals aggregate income. Consequently insofar as people's standard of living is influenced by their *income*, any change in aggregate expenditure will affect the standard of living. However, people's *current* living standards are also affected by the level of consumption (including government consumption). Since consumption can vary as a proportion of national income it follows that current living standards can vary at a given level of national income.

We saw in a previous chapter that it may be necessary to restrict the growth of consumption in order to free resources for the production of capital or investment goods. This has the effect of depressing current living standards in order to improve future living standards.

Consumption versus government consumption

In the above section we treated (private) consumption and government consumption together as contributing to the current standard of living. But many people argue that the two do not make the same contribution, pound for pound. There are, in fact, two conflicting sets of arguments. The first is usually advanced by left-wing economists, the second by right-wing, free market, economists:

1   A pound's worth of government consumption is worth *more* than a pound's worth of private consumption, for two reasons:
(*a*)   Government consumption is valued at cost, as noted above, i.e. it does not include the profit margins which 'inflate' the prices of goods included under private consumption.
(*b*)   Government consumption is, or at least can be, concentrated on the poorer, more needy members of the community.
2   A pound's worth of government consumption is worth *less* than a pound's worth of private consumption. We know that when consumers buy any product they must expect it to yield at least as much satisfaction as it costs. There is, however, no reason to believe that the satisfaction yielded by government consumption equals its cost, since consumers do not have to pay the full cost.

Exports versus domestic sales

Exports give rise to domestic incomes (wages, profits etc.). But the goods are purchased abroad and consequently do not contribute to the *current* standard of living of the country in which the goods and services are produced. However, the money derived from a surplus of exports over imports can be used to improve *future* living standards in two ways:

(a)   It can be used to finance a future excess of imports over exports, i.e. a higher level of purchases.
(b)   The money can be invested abroad in the various ways outlined in Chapter 14. These investments will yield a future stream of income which can be used to increase expenditure.

> **Qu. 16.2**   Do private and government consumption make the same contribution to the standard of living?

Other aspects of the standard of living

We have been concerned so far with expenditure on goods and services. But other factors influence the standard of living:

Economic bads

We have made several references in earlier chapters to the incidence of economic bads, e.g. pollution, loss of green spaces. Consequently we need do no more here than repeat the fact that economic bads serve to lower the standard of living.

Distribution of income

Figure 16.1 shows two alternative distributions of income. Curve A shows an absolutely equal distribution; for example 50 per cent of the population receives 50 per cent of income. Curve B, on the other hand, shows a highly unequal distribution; for example the lowest 50 per cent of income earners receive only 5 per cent of total income.

Because socialist and Marxist political philosophy has stressed equality, including equality of income, distribution A might be associated with economies at the command end of the spectrum, and distribution B with economies at the free market end.

At best this would be a simplification and at worst highly misleading. Evidence suggests that income (including income in kind such as free houses and cars) tends to be less equally distributed in some planned economies, such as the USSR, than in some economies with a large free market element. The most unequal distributions tend to be found not in modern industrialised economies but in

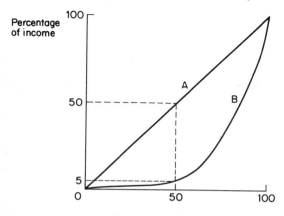

Fig. 16.1   Distribution of income

some less developed countries where political power and wealth are concentrated in a relatively few hands.

In most countries the distribution of income lies between the two extremes represented by curves A and B, partly as a result of government measures to re-distribute income. These measures, which are discussed in detail in the following chapter, include:

(*a*)   A progressive tax system, which requires people with high incomes to pay a bigger proportion of their income in tax than is paid by people with low incomes.

(*b*)   Forms of government spending which add more to the incomes of low than of high earners, e.g. unemployment benefit.

As an example of the re-distributive effects of government policy consider the table on page 180, which refers to the UK in 1984, and is based on data appearing in Economic Progress Report, December 1985, published by the Treasury.

The first column shows that the original income per person in the bottom fifth (quintile) of households was only one fiftieth (2 per cent) of the income per person in all households (given as 100). However, when cash benefits and taxes are taken into account, the income of the lowest earners was over one-half the average. Moreover, when benefits in kind (e.g. health and education) are taken into account, final income was almost three-quarters of the average.

Income per head of lowest and highest groups of households (Average household income per head = 100)

	Lowest quintile	Highest quintile
Original income	2	190
Income after cash benefits and taxes	59	157
Final income	73	143

On the other hand the effect of government policy was to move the highest income earners from an original income 90 per cent above average to a final income 43 per cent above average.

There is a continuing debate as to whether this degree of redistribution is right, whether it is too little, or too much. The extreme positions tend to be taken by people who are mainly influenced by political considerations. Some people advocate (at least when they are not in power) that governments should aim for an almost absolutely equal distribution. At the other extreme are people who believe that governments should do nothing to redistribute income since taxation, except to finance essential services such as defence, constitutes theft.

People who allow their political views to be tempered by economic considerations realise that a dilemma may exist. High rates of taxation, whether of individuals or firms, *may* have *disincentive* effects. People may work less hard, firms may invest less, fewer risks may be taken. As a result national income may grow less quickly. This could lead to a situation in which although income is redistributed in favour of the lowest income earners their incomes grow less quickly than they would have done had income not been redistributed.

Distribution of wealth

Wealth contributes to the standard of living in two ways:
(a)   As we saw in Chapter 12, a stock of wealth gives rise to a flow of income.
(b)   Wealth can act as a cushion to protect people against some of the consequences of misfortune, such as redundancy or prolonged sickness. This protection can give a sense of well-being.

Given these advantages, governments frequently adopt policies designed to redistribute wealth. Many of the points discussed above in connection with the redistribution of income, including the disagreements over the appropriate degree of redistribution, apply also to wealth.

A progressive system of taxation normally helps to redistribute wealth as well as income. But there are other measures that are especially important with regard to the redistribution of wealth:

(a) Taxes may be levied on wealth in the hands of the holder, or when wealth is transferred from one person to another, e.g. at death.
(b) The wider acquisition of wealth may be encouraged, e.g. by subsidising house purchase, by giving tax concessions on the purchase of shares and on contributions to pension policies. These items are becoming an increasingly important part of the wealth of many people.

> **Qu. 16.3** Discuss the proposition than an increase in national income must lead to an increase in the standard of living.
> **Qu. 16.4** Evaluate the case for government policies designed to redistribute income and wealth.

Employment and unemployment

As noted in earlier chapters, an increase in expenditure is associated with an increase in income and output. It is often also associated with an increase in employment and a fall in unemployment. However, there are two circumstances in which this may *not* be so:

An increase in labour productivity

We have shown in previous chapters that labour productivity may increase for several reasons, including an increase in the amount of capital (machinery, etc.) at the disposal of each worker, and learning by experience to work more efficiently. In many countries labour productivity increases by around three per cent each year. This means that if expenditure rises by less than 3 per cent (or whatever the rate of productivity increase is in the country in question), employment will fall. Moreover, other things being equal, unemployment will rise.

This situation can be illustrated by reference to the production possibility boundary. In Figure 16.2 (page 182) the boundary AB denotes economic capacity in period 1. To simplify this we assume that all resources are fully utilised, and that output is X. Productivity then increases so that the production possibility boundary

182   *Basic Economics*

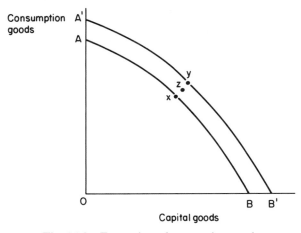

Fig. 16.2   Expansion of economic capacity

shifts in period 2 to $A^1 B^1$. To prevent a fall in employment, output would need to expand to Y (or to some other point on the new boundary). If an output of Z was sufficient to meet the new level of expenditure, there would be a fall in employment.

This situation may appear to cause a dilemma for governments if they can influence the rate of change in labour productivity, e.g. by granting tax concessions for investment. Should a government encourage an increase in labour productivity because of its potential advantage, i.e. an expansion of economic capacity which permits a higher level of expenditure, or should it discourage it because of the potential disadvantage, i.e. a possible rise in unemployment?

In practice most governments have taken the view that the dilemma is more apparent than real. An increase in labour productivity often leads to a fall in the real cost of production and thus enables producers to reduce their prices or at least to moderate the rate of price increase. If costs and prices rise less rapidly in one country than in others, that country will become more competitive internationally. It will be able to capture markets from its less efficient competitors, and more workers will be required to produce the additional output. On the other hand an attempt to maintain employment by restraining labour productivity will be self-defeating; the country will become less competitive and will lose markets.

An increase in the labour supply

If the labour supply is increasing, an increase in expenditure may be accompanied by an increase in both employment *and* unemployment. Such a situation existed in the UK in the late 1970s. Following a steep rise in the birth rate in the late 1950s, the 1970s saw a sharp increase in the number of school leavers. The increase in expenditure and output was insufficient to absorb all the additional people seeking work, and although the number in work increased in the 1970s, so too did the number of registered unemployed.

> **Qu. 16.5** In what circumstances may an increase in output *not* lead to a fall in the number of registered unemployed?
>
> **Qu. 16.6** Should the government encourage or discourage increases in labour productivity?

Measurement of unemployment

In the situation described in the previous section, it was possible to clearly identify an increase in unemployment, since the young people concerned registered as unemployed in order to:

(*a*)   receive benefit, and
(*b*)   obtain information about vacancies and be put in contact with employers.

It is less easy to identify what is happening if the unemployed do not register because they would not gain by so doing. In the UK in the 1980s a substantial number of married women left employment but did not register as unemployed because they did not qualify for benefit.

On the other hand, some of the registered unemployed may not be available for work, for various reasons. Some may, for medical reasons, be unable to fill the existing job vacancies. Others may be unwilling to take up employment.

It is, therefore, extremely difficult to make an accurate estimate of unemployment, and therefore of how well an economy is performing in this respect. Estimates of unemployment in the UK in 1985 ranged from 2·7 to 4·4 millions!

Employment and leisure

A fall in employment that is *not* accompanied by an increase in unemployment *may* be an extremely desirable development. Indeed, one of the signs of an increase in living standards is that people can afford to retire earlier, and to enjoy more leisure.

Inflation

Inflation usually means rising prices, although inflationary tendencies may exist even when prices are stable. This can be illustrated with reference to Figure 16.3 in which S is an aggregate, economy-wide, supply curve and D_1 shows the demand for all goods and services. The average price of goods and services is P_1 and output is Q_1.

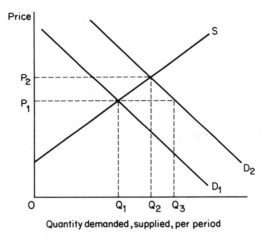

Fig. 16.3   Open and suppressed inflation

Increase in demand

When demand increases to D_2, one of two things can happen:

(*a*)   The operation of market forces leads to an increase in price to P_2 (and output to Q_2). This response we can call *open inflation*.

(*b*)   The government imposes controls to prevent prices from rising. As can be seen from Figure 16.3, if price is fixed at P_1, demand exceeds supply by Q_1Q_3, a situation termed *suppressed* or *repressed inflation*. The excess demand will manifest itself in shortages, queues and black market operations (charging prices above the official prices).

Since it is difficult to estimate the extent of suppressed inflation (if any), the rate of price increase is usually taken as the measure of inflation.

Inflation and the cost of living

In most countries information is published relating to changes in the prices of various groups of products, e.g. industrial materials, energy, wholesale prices and retail prices. Consumers are, of course, most interested in changes in the prices of the products that they buy. In the UK these changes are measured by the retail price index.

Retail price index

This index measures changes in the price of a 'basket' of goods and services bought by the 'average' consumer. Consumers are asked on a regular basis to record the percentage of their spending accounted for by various items, and these percentages are used as 'weights' in the construction of the (retail) price index. A highly simplified example of this procedure is given in the table below.

A Price Index

Product group	Weight	Price	Weighted price	Price	Weighted price
		Year 1	Year 1	Year 2	Year 2
Food	4	100	400	110	440
Clothes	3	100	300	90	270
Entertainment	3	100	300	105	315
			1000		1025

The weights attached to the three product groups are given in the first column. In year 1, the base year, the price of each product is set equal to 100. The weighted prices are obtained by multiplying each price index by the appropriate weight. The sum of the weighted prices is 1000.

In year 2 the price of food increases by 10 per cent (index 110), the price of clothes falls by 10 per cent (index 90) and the price of entertainment rises by 5 per cent (index 105). The sum of the weighted prices, obtained as before, is now 1025. With the index in year 1 at 1000, the index in year 2 is:

$$\frac{1025}{1000} \times 100 = 102 \cdot 5$$

In other words, the average price rise is $2 \cdot 5$ per cent.

Effects of inflation

We showed in Chapter 12 that the government might try to reduce aggregate expenditure in order to combat inflation. Why is inflation thought to be undesirable? In answering this question it is useful to distinguish between its internal and external effects.

Internal effects

These internal effects arise mainly because the rate of inflation cannot be predicted accurately, i.e. because of *uncertainty*. This uncertainty has two main consequences:

1 *It increases costs* If any market is to work efficiently, buyers and sellers must be well informed about prices. Inflation increases the costs that must be incurred in obtaining the information required to make good decisions.

This can be illustrated by the situation facing a housewife making her weekly purchases of groceries. She has a number of alternative shops from which she can buy her various requirements, and one of the factors influencing her decision is the price charged by each shop.

For many people this decision is difficult at the best of times, but it is far easier when prices are stable than when they are constantly changing, since the housewife can never be sure about the price changes made by each of the shops. To update her information takes time and effort.

The same principle applies to the decisions made by company purchasing officers. The more frequently prices are revised upwards (i.e. the higher is the rate of inflation), the more often purchasing officers have to obtain new price lists from potential suppliers.

2 *Windfall gains and losses* The term 'windfall' denotes that gains (or losses) are the result of chance rather than of rational calculation. Windfall gains and losses occur when transactions extend over time, as when money is loaned for, say, a year.

If inflation could be predicted accurately no windfall losses or gains would arise. For example assume that borrowers and lenders agree that a loan should attract a real rate of interest of 5 per cent a year. If there is no inflation, i.e. if prices are stable, the loan will be made at a nominal, and hence a real, interest rate of 5 per cent.

If lenders and borrowers expect prices to rise over the period of the loan by 5 per cent, the loan will be made at a nominal interest rate of 10 per cent, (the real rate again being 5 per cent).

In neither of these instances is there a windfall gain or loss, because it was possible to predict the rate of inflation. However, consider what happens when the rate of inflation is not predictable (the usual situation). For example everyone may expect prices to remain constant, and hence agree a nominal interest rate of 5 per cent, whereas prices actually rise by 5 per cent.

If a loan of £100 is made for a year, the lender at the end of the year receives £105, comprising repayment of the loan (£100) plus the agreed interest (£5). However, he finds that since prices have risen by 5 per cent he can buy with his £105 only as much as he could previously have bought with his £100. He has incurred costs (risk and lack of liquidity) for no return, i.e. he has suffered a windfall loss. The borrower, on the other hand, has obtained a windfall gain. Had prices fallen, the reverse would have happened. The lender would have benefited at the expense of the borrower.

The root of the above problem is that the contract between borrower and lender could not be revised to take account of the unexpected circumstances. Any revision that benefited the borrower would be to the disadvantage of the lender, and vice versa, and it would, therefore, be very difficult to reach agreement.

A similar principle applies to other contracts. For example the government might agree to increase state benefits, such as retirement pensions, annually, the increase to equal the rate of price increase in the previous year. This arrangement might be based on the assumption of a constant rate of inflation. If the rate of inflation were to suddenly rise, pensioners and other beneficiaries would suffer. They might, for example, receive a 5 per cent increase at the end of year 1, and then face a 15 per cent increase in prices in year 2. (Employed people are usually better able to negotiate wage and salary increases to compensate for unexpected price increases.) The disadvantages suffered by pensioners as a result of accelerating inflation in the UK in the mid-1970s led to a change in arrangements, with the rates of benefits being revised more frequently than previously.

External effects

By contrast with the internal effects considered above, the external effects of inflation apply whether or not the rate of inflation is accurately predicted. As noted above, if prices rise more rapidly in one country than in other countries that country is likely to lose markets, both at home and overseas, to its competitors. The fall in output leads to a fall in income and employment.

As we saw in the previous chapter, if imports exceed exports this is likely to cause a fall in the country's exchange rate. The fall in the exchange rate causes the price of exports to fall and of imports to rise, and hence helps to restore the country's international competitiveness. However, even if employment returns to its previous level, real income will not do so, since prices in the home market are higher than previously (see Chapter 14). Another way of expressing the new situation is that the country has to sell a bigger volume of exports than previously, to pay for a given volume of imports.

> **Qu. 16.7** Discuss (*a*) the internal, (*b*) the external, effects of inflation.
>
> **Qu. 16.8** Explain what you understand by (*a*) suppressed inflation, (*b*) the cost of living, (*c*) a regressive tax system, (*d*) windfall gains.

Balance of payments

A healthy balance of payments implies that the flow of money into a country from abroad *at least equals* the outflow of money to other countries. As we saw in Chapter 14, these financial flows have several sources: payment for goods and services, overseas investment, profits arising from previous investments, etc.

If a country has a persistent balance of payments deficit this is likely to have two effects:

(*a*) The exchange rate will fall, with the inflationary consequences outlined in the previous section.

(*b*) The country's foreign currency reserves will decline to a dangerously low level.

Consequently governments take corrective action to try to remedy a persistent deficit. Occasional deficits, on the other hand, are seldom a cause for concern. Indeed it would not be realistic for a country to aim at a persistent surplus, since this would imply a persistent deficit elsewhere in the international economy.

Economic capacity

As we saw in Chapter 12, an expansion of economic capacity is required for a sustained rise in national income. Consequently, although in evaluating performance in a given year attention may be focussed on the change in national income, a longer time perspective would require that equal attention should be given to changes in economic capacity.

Equality

We have already discussed equality in connection with the redistribution of income and wealth. But equality has numerous other aspects (some of which have a strong non-economic content). These include equality with respect to:

1 *Employment* As we noted in Chapter 2, differences in natural abilities mean that some people find it easier to obtain work than others. But governments may be able to lessen the disparities by providing training for unemployed workers and by encouraging firms to move to regions of heaviest unemployment.

2 *Education* By spending money on schools, colleges, etc., and by providing student grants, governments can try to ensure that no one is denied education because of a low household income.

3 *Health* Public spending can make medical services available to households who might not be able to afford these facilities.

Overall performance

We have considered seven main indicators of performance. As noted in the introduction, an evaluation of the overall performance of an economy would require weights to be attached to these various indicators. Different people would attach different weights, according to their personal circumstances, political beliefs, etc. Evaluations of the performance of a given economy can therefore differ markedly.

Differences in evaluation can arise even if the economy has moved in the same direction on all counts (e.g. expenditure, output, income and employment have all risen). Differences are even more likely to arise when, as often happens, there is a *trade-off* between one aspect of performance and another, when a better performance here means a less good performance elsewhere. We have already referred to some of these trade-offs, but to conclude the chapter we present a more comprehensive list of possible trade-offs.

1 *Unemployment and inflation* An increase in expenditure may reduce unemployment but increase inflation.

2 *Unemployment and balance of payments* An increase in expenditure may reduce unemployment but worsen the balance of payments.

3 *Current and future consumption* In order to release resources for investment, which will expand economic capacity and potential consumption in the future, it may be necessary to depress current consumption.

4 *Private versus government expenditure* In order to finance an increase in government expenditure it may be necessary to increase taxes, leading to a lower level of private expenditure. Also, increasing the resources devoted to government expenditure may impose a

limitation on the output of products for purchase by consumers and producers.

5   *Exports and domestic expenditure*   In order to increase exports it may be necessary to divert goods from the domestic (home) market.

6   *Increase and redistribution of income*   Although the evidence on this point is far from clear, it is possible that measures to redistribute income (or reduce other inequalities) could reduce the rate at which aggregate income grows.

These trade-offs are most likely to arise at a high level of capacity utilisation, when there are few unused resources, and could then be seen as a penalty of success. However, they can also arise at lower levels of capacity utilisation.

Qu. 16.9	Why might it be difficult to reach agreement about how well an economy has performed?
Qu. 16.10	Explain, with examples, what you understand by the term 'trade-off'.

17

Management of the Economy

Introduction

The management referred to in the title of this chapter is undertaken by government ministers and civil servants. They manage in the sense that they set objectives for the progress of the economy in very much the same way as the managers and directors of companies, and try to ensure that those objectives are achieved, especially by influencing demand. The objectives that might be set by governments are those that we have discussed in previous chapters, including:

(*a*) an increase in national income;
(*b*) a low (or zero) rate of inflation;
(*c*) a low level of unemployment;
(*d*) an expansion of economic capacity;
(*e*) a healthy balance of payments.

In the previous chapter we discussed the relationship between aggregate expenditure and these objectives, and it will be useful to summarise that discussion before discussing the various policies that might be adopted in order to influence aggregate expenditure.

In Figure 17.1, with aggregate demand D_1 and aggregate supply S, average price is P_1 and output is Q_1. If the government adopted measures to increase demand to D_2 output would increase to Q_2, indicating an increase in national income, a fall in unemployment and probably an expansion of economic capacity. Unfortunately the increase in demand also leads to inflation, price rising from P_1 to P_2. Moreover, it is likely to lead to a worsening of the balance of payments as the rise in price makes the country less competitive and as imports rise.

Two possibilities now arise. The first is that despite the increase in prices and deteriorating balance of payments the government is

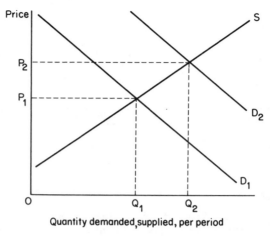

Fig. 17.1 Increase in output and price

able, if it wishes, to maintain expenditure D_2 and output Q_2. In other words the government can choose to accept inflation and a deteriorating balance of payments as the price that must be paid for higher income, output and employment.

The second possibility is that the government does *not* have this choice. For one reason or another, perhaps the fear of entering an inflationary spiral or of the country's foreign exchange reserves becoming exhausted, the government may feel obliged to bring expenditure back to its previous level. Although economists often disagree about precisely how effective demand management policies can be, there is a large measure of agreement that a country can no longer 'spend its way out of a recession'. We discuss the implications of this fact towards the end of the chapter.

> **Qu. 17.1** Why is it believed that a country can no longer spend its way out of recession?

We discuss below the policies that might be adopted to influence demand or expenditure, but first it will be useful to review the components of aggregate expenditure.

Aggregate expenditure

As we showed in the previous chapter, aggregate expenditure is the sum of consumption, investment, government consumption and exports (minus imports). The government can attempt to influence aggregate expenditure (and hence the rate of inflation, the level of unemployment, etc.) by influencing any of these expenditure flows. It may attempt to exert influence through three sets of policies: *fiscal policy*, *monetary policy* and *direct controls*. We discuss each of these in turn, beginning with fiscal policy.

Fiscal policy

There are two sides to fiscal policy: *taxation* and *government expenditure*. Taxation reduces expenditure, government expenditure increases it, and the overall effect depends upon the balance between revenue from taxation and government expenditure. We consider this balance later in the chapter, but first we discuss the two sides in turn, beginning with government expenditure.

Government expenditure

General (i.e. central plus local) government expenditure comprises:

(*a*)   expenditure on goods and services;
(*b*)   transfer payments.

Expenditure on goods and services
This also comprises two forms of spending:

(*a*)   Consumption spending.
(*b*)   Investment spending.

We have explained the distinction between these two forms of spending in earlier chapters, and it is sufficient here to give a simple illustration. The provision of certain types of medical services requires investment (or capital) spending, e.g. building and equipping hospitals, and consumption (or current) spending, e.g. paying the salaries of doctors, nurses and administrators.

Both forms of spending generate output and income. (As we shall see below, this is *not* true of spending on transfer payments.)

The pattern of expenditure on goods and services
The pattern varies from one country to another, but there is often a strong emphasis on the *infrastructure*. Important areas in many countries include:

1   Defence and internal security
2   Health
3   Education

4   Housing
5   Transport and communications
6   Social services (used, for example, by the elderly and disabled).

As we showed in Chapter 9, the basic reason for the provision of services by the state is the belief that they would be under-provided by the private sector. Looking at the matter from another point of view, consumption would be too low because:

(a)   Private producers would need to charge a price that covered their costs and yielded a profit (see the discussion of merit goods in Chapter 9).
(b)   Private producers would not be able to finance the production of public goods (see Chapter 9).

Transfer payments

In developed countries governments make a wide range of transfer payments, including social security benefits (e.g. retirement pensions, unemployment benefit), grants and loans to individuals (e.g. to students attending college), and grants and loans to firms (e.g. subsidies for the purchase of machinery or for training programmes).

Transfer payments, whatever their form, are *not* made in exchange for the production of goods and services, and so they do not *directly* contribute to aggregate expenditure and output. (However, they contribute indirectly, when they are subsequently spent by the recipients.) Indeed, the term indicates that income is *transferred* from the government (in fact from taxpayers and ratepayers) to the unemployed, pensioners, etc.

> **Qu. 17.2**   Why is it important to distinguish between government expenditure on goods and services and transfer payments?

Taxation

We consider the objectives of taxation below. But it will be helpful first to describe the various forms of taxation.

A broad distinction can be made between direct taxes and indirect or expenditure taxes.

Direct taxes

Direct taxes are taxes levied on the income or wealth of individuals and institutions. Different countries may adopt different taxes, but these usually include taxes on:

(*a*)   Personal income derived from employment.
(*b*)   Other forms of personal income, e.g. dividends, interest.
(*c*)   Profits earned by companies.
(*d*)   Wealth. A tax may be levied on the total wealth held by an individual or on certain forms of wealth, e.g. in many countries local authorities levy taxes on the value of buildings owned by individuals or institutions. (In the UK this tax is known as rates.) In some instances a tax is levied when wealth is transferred, e.g. in the UK an inheritance tax is levied on wealth transferred at, or a few years before, death.

Indirect or expenditure taxes

In principle a tax could be levied on the basis of an individual's total expenditure within a given period, e.g. a year. In practice indirect taxes are imposed on *products*. The more that is bought of a given product, the more is paid in tax. As noted in Chapter 5, there are two types of expenditure tax:

(*a*)   *Ad valorem* taxes. The tax is related to the selling price of the product; the higher the price the greater the amount of tax per unit. A good example is value added tax, levied by all members of the European Community.
(*b*)   Specific taxes. The tax is levied at a given amount per unit sold, regardless of the selling price (although if prices rise over time, the rate of tax is often raised). Examples include the excise duties levied in the UK on petrol, tobacco, and alcoholic drinks.

Social security contributions

In many countries social security benefits are financed partly from general taxation, but mainly from social security contributions. These contributions can be seen, in effect, as a form of taxation. They have two parts:

(*a*)   The employee's contribution, which may be levied at either a flat or a graduated rate. It acts very much like personal income tax.
(*b*)   The employer's contribution, which may be levied at a fixed amount per employee or may be related to the total wage and salary bill. This is, in effect, a form of payroll tax, a tax on the use of labour.

> **Qu. 17.3** Explain how fiscal policy can influence the level of aggregate expenditure.

Objectives of taxation

Having described the main forms of taxation we now consider the reasons why taxes may be levied. These include:

(a)   Raising revenue to finance government expenditure.
(b)   Influencing the pattern of expenditure.
(c)   Redistributing income and wealth.

As we discuss each of these purposes or objectives we shall see that conflicts may arise; a tax that contributes to one objective may make it more difficult to achieve another.

Financing government expenditure

The primary purpose of taxation is to raise the revenue required to finance government expenditure. If this was the only consideration, a structure of taxation would be required in which tax was paid by as many people, and on as many transactions as possible. In many countries the taxation net is cast wide, but the system does not extend to every person and transaction.

For example in the UK personal income tax yields the greatest revenue and is paid by the majority of adults. However, a system of allowances ensures that income tax is not paid by the lowest income earners. Also in the UK value added tax and other expenditure taxes are imposed on most goods and services. But no tax is imposed on some necessities, such as basic foodstuffs, which form a large part of the expenditure of poorer families.

Influencing the pattern of expenditure

This objective is mainly met via indirect taxation. It is possible to discourage the consumption of products such as alcoholic drinks, tobacco and petrol by imposing high taxes. Governments may adopt this policy for two reasons:

(a)   Heavy consumption is believed to be bad for the consumers. For example, most people accept that there is a clear link between smoking and various forms of ill-health, and that excessive drinking can cause physical, mental and emotional damage.
(b)   Consumption gives rise to costs which are borne by others than the consumers of the product. The cost of medical treatment for people suffering from lung cancer or alcoholism is borne by the state. Similarly, car drivers can injure not only themselves but also pedestrians.

Taxes imposed to restrict consumption can also contribute to the first objective, raising revenue. But this is not always so. Taxes may be raised to a level at which the revenue, or yield, falls.

In Figure 17.2, with the initial supply and demand curves, S_1 and D, Q_1 is bought at price P_1. After the imposition of a tax P_1P_2 per unit, price rises to P_2, at which Q_2 is bought. Tax revenue is shown by the rectangle P_1P_2AB. An increase in the tax rate to P_1P_3 would result in a price of P_3 at which Q_3 would be bought. Tax revenue, now shown by the rectangle P_1P_3CE, would be less than it was previously.

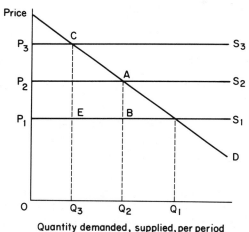

Fig. 17.2 Fall in tax revenue

Governments try to predict the effects of proposed tax changes. This requires an estimate to be made of the price elasticity of demand, as noted in Chapter 6.

The pattern of expenditure can also be influenced by imposing low or even zero taxes on other products. As noted above, basic foodstuffs are not taxed in many countries.

Redistributing income and wealth
In order to achieve this objective a taxation structure is required which will produce the following results:

1 The highest direct taxes are levied on persons having the highest incomes and holding most wealth. Since we discussed this point in detail in Chapter 16, we need not repeat the arguments for and against high tax rates. But two additional points can be made. First, in most countries taxes on the highest incomes can contribute only a

small part of the government's required revenue, since they can be levied on so few people. Second, taxation of company profits is limited by the need to allow companies to retain sufficient profits to finance future growth.

2   The heaviest indirect taxes are levied on products of greatest relative importance in the spending of richer people. The disadvantage of this measure is that the costs of administration may soak up most of any extra revenue obtained from the higher taxes. Additional costs are incurred, by firms and by the government, in administering a multi-rate system. Moreover consumers' reactions may mean that the system has to be adjusted frequently if it is to be effective. For example assume that the government decides to levy a heavy tax on yachts. This may lead consumers to buy fewer yachts and to spend more on luxury holidays. Furthermore if the government then levies a high tax on holidays, e.g. by introducing a special tax on hotel accommodation, consumers may evade this by taking holidays abroad!

> **Qu. 17.4**   Give two objectives of taxation and explain how these objectives might best be achieved.

Progressive and regressive taxation

When discussing the forms of taxation we referred to the effects of individual taxes on various income groups. Governments are also concerned about the impact of the *tax system as a whole*. A system is progressive if people with high incomes pay a higher proportion of their income in tax than people with low incomes. A system is regressive if the reverse applies.

The UK has a progressive system of direct taxation, but a mildly regressive system of indirect taxation. Overall the tax system is mildly progressive.

> **Qu. 17.5**   Explain what is meant by a progressive tax system, and outline (*a*) the advantages, (*b*) the disadvantages of such a system.

Taxation and real income

As noted in Chapter 10, real income indicates a person's purchasing power, and depends upon nominal or money income and the prices of goods and services. Taxation reduces real income in two ways:

(*a*)   Direct taxes reduce nominal income; since prices are unchanged they also reduce real income.

(*b*)   Indirect taxes cause an increase in prices. Since nominal income is unchanged, real income falls.

Government spending, taxation and aggregate expenditure

We have shown that government spending increases aggregate expenditure, either directly or indirectly, and that taxation reduces expenditure. The overall impact on aggregate expenditure depends upon the balance of government spending and taxation.

Balanced budget

This term indicates that government spending equals revenue from taxation. It might be thought that a balanced budget would leave aggregate expenditure unchanged. But in fact it is more likely to result in an increase in expenditure, as illustrated in the table below.

Balanced Budget

	£ billions	Effect on aggregate expenditure (£ billions)
Government expenditure on goods and services	100	100
Transfer payments	100	95
Total government expenditure	200	195
Revenue from taxation	200	−170
		25

Government expenditure and tax revenue are both £200 billions. The expenditure of £100 billions on goods and services contributes directly to aggregate expenditure. Transfer payments contribute to expenditure as and when they are spent by the recipients. Since many of the recipients are on low incomes, a high proportion will be spent; we have assumed 95 per cent, giving an expenditure of £95 billions.

Revenue from taxation is £200 billions. However, it is unlikely that this will cause an equal fall in expenditure. Taxpayers will reduce expenditure by less than this, making up the difference by reducing their saving. We assume that saving is reduced by £30 billions, leaving a reduction in expenditure (consumption and investment) of £170 billions.

The overall effect is an increase in aggregate expenditure of £25 billions. We discuss the possible significance of this outcome below. But first we consider briefly the situation where the budget is *not* balanced.

Budget deficit

A budget deficit indicates that government expenditure exceeds revenue from taxation. A budget deficit is likely to cause an even bigger increase in expenditure than a balanced budget.

Budget surplus

A budget surplus indicates that revenue from taxation exceeds government expenditure. A modest budget surplus could leave aggregate expenditure unchanged. However, there must clearly be a point where the surplus of tax revenue over government expenditure is so great as to cause aggregate expenditure to fall.

> **Qu. 17.6**   Give arithmetic examples to illustrate the effects on expenditure of (*a*) a budget deficit, (*b*) a budget surplus.

Fiscal policy and optimum expenditure

We have shown above that it may be difficult to determine what the best or optimum level of expenditure is, if only because a change in expenditure can have different effects on different variables, such as unemployment and inflation. However, let us assume that the government has decided what level of *aggregate* expenditure would be best. In order to arrive at the appropriate balance between government expenditure and taxation, the government needs to estimate the likely size of the other spending flows: consumption, investment and exports (minus imports).

Monetary policy

Monetary policy consists of measures intended to influence the cost and availability of money. (It may be useful at this point to refresh your memory by re-reading the section in Chapter 3 on money and credit.) Figure 17.3 provides a framework within which we subsequently place the various measures that a government might adopt.

In Figure 17.3, D denotes the demand for money. Money is demanded for various purposes, including financing expenditure on goods and services. The shape of the curve indicates that the more expensive it is to acquire money, i.e. the higher the rate of interest, the less money is demanded. This will in turn be reflected in lower planned expenditure.

The initial supply curve is S_1, indicating that Q_1 money would be supplied at any rate of interest. Supply will be fixed in this way if the

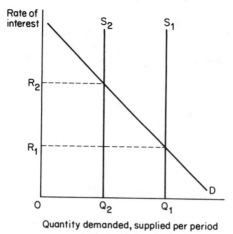

Fig. 17.3 Changing money supply and rate of interest

monetary authorities (the central bank and the government) are able to control the money supply. If the authorities are not able to exercise this control, we would expect the supply curve to slope up from left to right, indicating that people are willing and able to lend more at higher rates of interest.

Given demand D and supply S_1, the rate of interest is R_1, and the quantity demanded and supplied is Q_1. If the authorities wish to reduce the level of expenditure, they might try to reduce the quantity of money demanded to Q_2.

They could attempt to engineer this change in one of two ways:

1 A reduction in the supply of money to S_2 would cause an increase in the rate of interest to R_2 and a fall in the quantity demanded to Q_2.
2 An increase in the rate of interest to R_2 would cause the quantity demanded to fall to Q_2, and supply would fall in line (S_2).

We now consider the various measures that might be adopted under each approach.

Reduction in the supply of money

The authorities might bring about a fall in the supply of money in several ways:

(*a*) By issuing instructions. For example the banks might be instructed to reduce their lending by 10 per cent.

(b)   By regulating the banks' balance-sheet ratios. In Chapter 3 we showed that banks learn from experience that they can lend a multiple of the money initially deposited with them, and that this lending increases the money supply. The authorities may enforce a lower multiple than the banks would wish to maintain, e.g. eight rather than the ten assumed in Chapter 3. Enforcing a lower multiple restricts the banks' ability to lend.

(c)   The authorities may reduce the base on which the banks' lending depends. (To discuss how the authorities might do this would take us beyond the scope of this book.)

Increase in the rate of interest

Measures that can be adopted under this heading include the following:

(a)   The central bank raises the rate of interest at which it makes money available to the banking system. To compensate for their higher costs, the commercial banks increase their lending rates.

(b)   The authorities instruct the banks to charge a higher rate of interest. (This measure is most likely to be adopted in a command economy.)

(c)   The authorities persuade the banks to increase interest rates on the ground that this is in the public interest.

Expansionary monetary policy

We have discussed the measures that might form part of a restrictive monetary policy. But monetary policy is not always restrictive. On some occasions the authorities wish to encourage expenditure, and therefore adopt measures to increase the availability of money and reduce its cost.

We need not discuss these measures in detail since they are virtually the reverse of those discussed above. However, they may not form a perfect 'mirror image'. For example although the authorities can instruct the banks to reduce their lending, they would be more likely to *encourage* rather than *instruct* them to increase their lending.

Monetary policy and the pattern of expenditure

We saw above that fiscal policy can have a strong impact on the pattern of expenditure, e.g. the sales of individual products can be affected by the imposition of indirect taxes. Monetary policy has a more neutral effect on expenditure. However, it appears that its impact may be greatest with respect to investment expenditure, especially the following two types:

(*a*) Expenditure by small firms. When money is 'tight', banks may cut back their lending to small firms rather than to their larger, more important customers.

(*b*) Expenditure by firms wishing to expand rapidly. Almost as a matter of definition, these firms are more likely to depend on borrowing than firms which have more modest ambitions.

Where policy is implemented via instructions the authorities may have more scope for 'fine-tuning'. For example in the past when the authorities have instructed the banks to restrict their lending they have sometimes exempted lending for certain purposes, e.g. to finance investment and exports. This indicates the authorities' concern with two of the objectives mentioned in the introduction: the expansion of economic capacity and a sound balance of payments.

> **Qu. 17.7** In what ways might a government attempt to influence the availability and cost of money?

Effectiveness of demand management policies: summary

We have shown that fiscal and monetary policy can both be used to change the level of aggregate expenditure. In the previous chapter we showed that an increase in aggregate expenditure may be associated with an increase in national income, a fall in unemployment and an expansion of economic capacity.

However, we have also shown that an increase in expenditure can have two undesirable consequences: an increase in the rate of inflation and a worsening of the balance of payments. These disadvantages limit the effectiveness of fiscal and monetary policy. Although there are different views about precisely how effective these policies can be, it is generally agreed, as noted above, that it is not possible for a country to spend its way out of a recession. Even the strongest advocates of such a policy recognise that it would need to be supplemented by other policies, including *direct controls*. Two main forms of control have been advocated: on prices and incomes and on imports.

Prices and incomes policies

It is argued that if prices could be controlled, it would be possible to increase expenditure and to run the economy with a high degree of capacity utilisation (including a low level of unemployment), but without a high level of inflation. In Figure 17.4 with demand D_1 and supply S, the initial price is P_1 and output Q_1. In the absence of controls, an increase in demand to D_2 would lead to a rise in price to P_2, at which output would be Q_2. However, if prices could be controlled, it would be possible to produce Q_3 at price P_1.

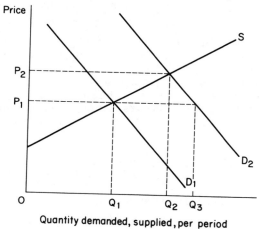

Fig. 17.4   Price control

Although the ultimate objective is to prevent increases in the price of goods and services, governments have often felt it necessary to control incomes (wages, salaries, dividends, etc.) as well. This reduces the danger that firms' costs might rise at a faster rate than the permitted rate of price increase, causing profits to fall to an unsatisfactory level. (Note that if this happened, output would probably fall, leaving an excess demand, giving rise to inflationary tendencies.) Against the potential advantages of prices and incomes policies must be put three disadvantages:

1   *High administration costs*   These costs are borne partly by the government and partly by firms, e.g. in preparing applications for price increases, in submitting wage agreements for approval. The more widespread the controls, the greater the costs of administration. (The difficulties involved in controlling the prices of some products, e.g. fresh foodstuffs, has often led to their being exempted from control.)

2   *Obtaining public support*   For controls to work effectively in a

democratic society a wide measure of popular support is required. In some countries, including the UK, the traditional antagonism between employers and employee representatives has made it extremely difficult to obtain this support, and the policy has eventually broken down as one side or the other has withdrawn its support.

Even before this point arrives, the policy may gradually lose its effectiveness, partly because the parties find ways round the regulations. For example, above-average wage increases may be allowed if they are accompanied by an agreement to increase productivity. In practice productivity increases foreshadowed in such agreements frequently do not occur. Moreover, it is alleged that the parties to an agreement know at the time that this is likely to happen.

It is easy to see why employees would support such an agreement, since they obtain higher wages. It is less easy to see why employers lend their support, if they know that productivity is unlikely to rise. But they may feel it necessary to pay the higher wages to retain sufficient labour. Moreover, they may expect to be allowed to increase their prices to compensate for at least part of any increase in their costs.

3 *Controls blunt the allocative function of the price mechanism* A broad-brush approach is usually adopted to the control of prices and incomes, e.g. it may be specified that no prices should rise for six months. (We have shown that some exceptions may be granted, but the more flexible the policy, the more costly it is to administer.) Although this approach has the advantage of simplicity, it prevents prices from responding to changes in demand and supply.

If there is an excess demand for certain products, a higher price and profit margin will attract resources into that market and supply will expand to match the demand. Price controls inhibit this process. The same argument applies to labour and other resources. A shortage of a given type of labour will be corrected more quickly the faster wages are allowed to rise.

These disadvantages have meant that a rigid system of controls is seen in most countries as being something to be imposed very much as a last resort, e.g. if the country appears to be entering an inflationary 'spiral', with the rate of price increases accelerating. In other circumstances different methods of influencing prices and incomes are usually advocated, including a tax-based income policy. Under this policy the government would announce a target or norm for wage increases. Employers would be free to offer higher increases if they wished, but would be taxed on any increase above the norm.

Qu. 17.8   Evaluate the case for a prices and incomes policy.

Controls on imports

We saw in Chapter 14 that temporary import controls are some-times justified on the grounds that the protection enables the industry concerned to increase its efficiency and subsequently compete successfully on an equal footing.

A similar argument has been advanced to justify economy-wide controls. The government would then be able to boost expenditure without the danger of a balance of payments deficit. This increase would lead to a 'virtuous circle', with producers being encouraged to undertake additional investment, leading to an expansion of economic capacity. Since investment in new products and processes would make the economy more competitive, there would be no reason to expect balance of payments problems to recur once the import controls are lifted.

This is illustrated in Figure 17.5 With demand D_1 and supply S_1 the initial price is P_1 and output Q_1. Demand then increases to D_2 and the increase in efficiency causes the supply curve to shift to S_2. The result is that price remains at P_1, and output increases to Q_2. (The shift in the supply curve might not be exactly as in Figure 17.5, and the new price could be either above or below the initial price.)

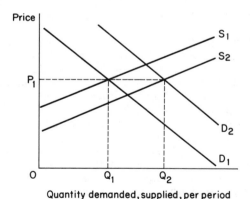

Fig. 17.5   Change in demand and supply

Although this scenario may appear attractive, it has two serious drawbacks:

(*a*)   As noted in Chapter 14, 'temporary' controls often turn out to have a much longer life than expected. With this in mind, other countries may retaliate by imposing controls.

(*b*) There is no guarantee that producers will take advantage of the protection to increase their efficiency. On the contrary they may feel that it is *less* important to be efficient, especially if they expect the protection to be continued.

Supply-side economics

Throughout this discussion measures to influence *demand* have been seen as the central plank of government policy, although other measures to supplement demand management policies have also been discussed. Even when policy resulted in a change in supply conditions, as in Figures 17.4 and 17.5, an increase in demand was the crucial measure.

It has generally become accepted in recent years that governments should give more attention than previously to measures to change the conditions of *supply*. The potential benefits of these measures are illustrated in Figure 17.6. With demand D, a shift of the supply curve from S_1 to S_2 would result in a fall in price from P_1 to P_2 and an increase in output from Q_1 to Q_2. (In fact if these measures were combined with an increase in demand to D^1, it would be possible to increase output to Q_3 at the initial price.)

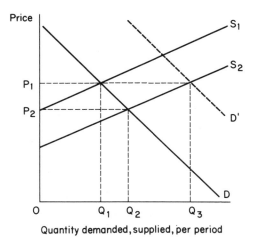

Fig. 17.6 Change in supply conditions

Measures that the government might adopt in order to try to shift the supply curve from S_1 to S_2 include:

1 *Legislation to reduce the power of the trade unions* We noted in Chapter 10 that trade unions may cause costs to be higher than they need be, e.g. by restricting the supply of labour or by negotiating higher wage rates.

2 *Reductions in state benefits to the unemployed* If some unemployed people are qualified to occupy vacant jobs but prefer to live on state benefits, reducing the level of benefit might persuade them to take employment.

3 *Increased expenditure on training and re-training* This would focus on those skills for which there is excess demand.

4 *Measures to increase geographical mobility* If there are labour shortages in some parts of the country and surpluses in others, a better balance between demand and supply can be achieved by:

(*a*) Providing more information about vacancies to workers, and about surplus labour to employers.

(*b*) Encouraging other workers to move to areas of labour shortage e.g. by paying removal expenses.

5 *A more vigorous competition policy* This would aim to increase efficiency and remove barriers to the entry of new firms (see Chapter 9).

Further Questions

1 List five characteristics of economic decisions.
2 Define and explain the significance of (a) scarcity, (b) opportunity cost.
3 'Since life is full of uncertainties, there is no point in making plans.' Discuss.
4 Define optimum population and explain why the optimum population of a country may change.
5 Mr Jones has a large farm on part of which he grows a range of vegetables, and on the rest of which he grazes sheep. How might the proportion of land devoted to these two uses be affected by each of the following: (a) a fall in the price of woollen cloth; (b) an increase in the demand for vegetables; (c) a rise in the price of weedkiller?
6 Comment on the proposition that an increase in profit margins will always lead to an increase in the rate of return.
7 Why is the time period under consideration likely to affect (a) elasticity of demand, (b) elasticity of supply?
8 How might a fall in the price of labour affect the quantity employed of (a) labour, (b) capital?
9 Distinguish between free market, command and mixed economies, giving examples of each, and explain why most economies are mixed.
10 Why is it sometimes suggested that the term 'work' should be re-defined?
11 Why is it that some occupations with poor working conditions have low wage rates?
12 What do the advertisements issued by banks and building societies tell us about competition to attract (a) borrowers, (b) savers?
13 What is meant when people say that Germany is richer than Britain?

14 Explain what is meant by (*a*) net investment, (*b*) human capital, (*c*) intermediate technology.
15 Explain the circumstances in which international trade will *not* take place.
16 Are trade barriers ever justified?
17 Discuss how the creation of a customs union might affect economic welfare.
18 Should the UK leave the EEC?
19 Explain why and how a government might seek to increase aggregate supply.
20 What difficulties do governments face in managing the economy?

Index

acid rain 103–4
advertising 4, 92–3, 94
aggregate expenditure (demand) 174, 191–3, 199

balance of payments 158–9, 165, 188, 191
bank
  assets 29, 128
  central 128–9
  commercial 127–8
  deposits 29, 30
  liabilities 29, 128
  loans 29, 30
  merchant 125
Bank for International Settlements 167
banking systems 28–30, 127–9
barriers
  to new entry 95
  to trade 159–63, 170
barter 25
benefits
  external 105–7
  private 105
bilateral trade 150–2
birth rate 12–13
bonds (gilt-edged) 126
borrowing 121–2
  government 126–7
budget
  balanced 199
  constraint 31, 35
  deficit 200
  surplus 200
business organisations
  private sector 76–8
  public sector 79–81

capital
  circulating (working) 18
  factor of production 17–19, 140–1
  fixed 17
  human 141
  market 123–5
  mobility 20, 21
  social 18
chain of production and distribution 24, 87–8
choice 2
Common Market (EEC) 171–3
companies 77–8
comparative advantage 22–3, 148–50
competition
  definition 91
  effects 94–5
  forms 91–4
complementary products 35
conglomerate merger 96
consumer sovereignty 71, 72
consumption 135, 174, 177
  alternative paths 142
  conspicuous 42
co-operatives 74, 82
cost
  average 45–50
  external 72, 100–5
  fixed 46
  opportunity 2, 52, 115
  private 100
  training 115–17
countertrade 25
credit
  cards 122
  creation 28–9
  trade 122
customs union 171, 173

death rate 13
debentures 122, 123, 131
deflation 157
demand
    aggregate 174, 191–3, 199
    curve 33, 34, 35, 39, 40–2, 56–8
        aggregate 206, 207
        currency 152–4
        labour 111
        perverse 41–2
    derived 65
    excess 56
    schedule 32
demerit goods 106
depreciation 18, 19, 141
    allowances 126
devaluation 157
dirty floating 155
diseconomies of scale 85–6
disequilibrium 56–8, 133–4, 154, 155
dissaving 135
diversification 10, 88
dominant suppliers 96–7
double
    coincidence of wants 25
    counting 131

economic
    aid 169, 170–1
    bads 145, 178
    capacity 136–8, 140, 141, 182, 191,
        206
    decisions
        benefits 3, 4, 7, 11
        characteristics 2
        costs 3, 4, 7
        governments 10–11
        households 3–8
        producers 8–10
    development 139–40, 145–7, 168
        strategies 146–7
    growth 138, 140, 143–5
    welfare 96–7
economies of scale 47, 82–4
    external 89
economy (economic system)
    classification 70
    command (planned) 72–5
    free market 60, 71–2
    mixed 75
efficiency 74, 98, 137, 163, 173
employers' organisations 119
employment 181–3
entrepreneurial activity 71
equality 188–9

equilibrium
    exchange rate 153–5
    factor market 68–9
    output 55, 79–80
    price 55, 56, 57, 63, 79–80
    rate of interest 201–2
European Economic Community 171–3
exchange 23–5
    international 150–2
    rate 151, 152–7, 188
        equilibrium 153–5
        fixed 155–6
        floating 155
exports 78, 153–5, 174, 178
external
    benefits 105–7
    costs 72, 100–5

finance
    government 126–7, 196
    households 121–2
    producers 122–5
fiscal policy 193–200
foreign currency reserves 159, 188
free
    -rider problem 107
    trade area 171
full employment 136

General Agreement on Tariffs and
    Trade (GATT) 164–5
government
    consumption 174, 177, 193
    expenditure on goods and services
        135, 193–4
    finance 126–7
    grants 117, 194
    transfer payments 194
growth of firms 88–9

horizontal growth (expansion, merger)
    88, 95

imports 153–5, 174
    controls 206–7
income
    distribution 145, 178–9
    elasticity of demand 37–9
    flow 130, 132
    national 131, 132–3, 141, 174–8, 191
        equilibrium 133, 134–5
        per head 141
        real 175–6, 188, 198
    redistribution 173, 179–80, 197–8
infant industry 163

inferior good 36–7, 38, 39
inflation 136, 137, 184–5
  effects 186–8, 191
  suppressed (repressed) 184
information 4, 39, 113–14, 160
infrastructure 131, 193
innovation 97
insurance companies 125–6
intermediate technology 147
International Bank for Reconstruction
  and Development (World Bank)
  166–7
international debt 169
International Development Association
  167
International Finance Corporation 167
International Monetary Fund (IMF)
  165–6, 168
investment 18, 135, 174, 177, 206
  trusts 126

labour
  factor of production 12–14
  mobility 20
  supply 108–13
land
  factor of production 16–17
  mobility 20, 21
learning 23
  effect 84–5
leisure 119, 144–5, 183
less developed countries (LDCs) 142,
  146–7, 165, 166, 167, 169, 170, 179
licensing 103
local authorities 81
luxuries 38

market
  capital 123–5
  factor 65
  new issue 123–4
  unlisted securities 125
mergers (takeovers) 95–6
  legislation 99–100
merit goods 106
migration 13
monetary policy 200–203
money
  characteristics 27
  demand 200–201
  forms 26
  functions 26
  near (quasi) 30
  supply 200–202
Monopolies Commission 99–100

monopoly 96–8
  legislation 99–100
multilateral trade 152
multinational companies 78

national debt 127
nationalised industries 81
necessities 38
new products 4, 9, 53, 72, 143
normal goods 35–6, 38, 39

opportunity cost 2, 52, 115

partnership 77
pension funds 125
planned expenditure 133–5, 200–201
planning 2
  by governments 10–11, 72–3
  by households 3–4, 31–2
  by producers 8–9, 42–3
population
  optimum 14
  size 12–14
  structure 15
pollution 102–4, 145, 178
price
  elasticity of demand 60–4
  elasticity of supply 64–5
  equilibrium (market clearing) 55, 56,
    57, 63, 79–80
  indicator of quality 42
prices and incomes policies 203–5
primary (extractive) industries 90
production possibility boundary 136–8,
  149, 181
productivity 10, 51, 140, 181–2
  diminishing 66–7
profit 45
  margins 48–50, 52, 63
  monopoly 96–7
  undistributed 126
property (ownership) rights 101–3
public
  corporations 81
  goods 106–7
  ownership 79–80

quotas 161, 162

rate of interest 201–2
regional trade groupings 171
resources
  allocation 70, 72, 97
  alternative combinations 10
  alternative uses 1

resources – *cont*.
  human 12–16
  mobility 19–21
  non-human 16–19
  ownership 70
  quality 14, 17, 19, 140–1
  quantity 12–14, 16, 18, 140
  reallocation 58–60
  unused 137, 141
  utilisation 99
Restrictive Practices
  Court 99
  legislation 98–9
retail price index 185
revaluation (upvaluation) 157

saving
  companies 126
  government 127
  households 122, 135
scarcity 2
secondary industries 90
shareholders 125–6
shares 122, 123, 131
small firms 86
social security contributions 195
sole traders 76–7
Special Drawing Rights (SDRs) 165, 168
specialisation 22–3, 149–50, 171, 173
standard of living 176–80
stock exchange 123
subsidy 53, 105, 117, 194
substitutes (substitution) 10, 33, 43, 61, 66, 94
supply
  curve 45, 47–50, 52, 53, 56–8, 62–4, 67–9, 80, 101–3
    aggregate 206, 207
    currency 152–4
    labour 108–13
  excess 56–7, 113
  inadequate 73
  -side economics 207–8

takeovers, *see* mergers

tariffs 161, 162, 165
tax
  ad valorem 53, 195
  direct 194–5, 197–8
  expenditure (indirect) 52–3, 63, 195, 196–7, 198
  specific 53, 195
  value added 53, 173
taxation
  disincentive effect 180
  forms 194–5
  objectives 196–8
  progressive 179, 198
  regressive 198
tertiary industries 90
trade
  gap 152, 153, 154
  -off 32, 189–90
  unions 117
training 14, 20, 11, 115–17
transfer
  earnings 109
  payments 194
Treasury Bills 126–7

uncertainty 2, 114, 186
underwriting 124
underemployment 146
unemployment 181, 191
  hidden 74
  measurement 183
unit trusts 126

vertical growth (expansion, merger) 88, 95
voluntary export restraints 161–2

wage 109
wealth 130–1
  distribution 145
  re-distribution 180–1, 197–8
windfall gains and losses 186–7
World Bank (International Bank for Reconstruction and Development) 166–7
work, definitions 119